Twelve Tales Untold

A *Study Guide*
for Ecumenical Reception

Edited by

John T. Ford *and* Darlis J. Swan

William B. Eerdmans Publishing Company
Grand Rapids, Michigan

Copyright © 1993 by Wm. B. Eerdmans Publishing Co.
255 Jefferson Ave. S.E., Grand Rapids, Mich. 49503
All rights reserved

Printed in the United States of America

Library of Congress Cataloging-in-Publication Data

Twelve tales untold: a study guide for ecumenical reception / edited by
John T. Ford and Darlis J. Swan.

p.   cm.

Includes bibliographical references.

ISBN 0-8028-0553-1

1. Ecumenical movement—Case studies. 2. Baptism and Christian
union—Case studies. 3. Lord's Supper and Christian union—Case
studies. 4. Pastoral theology and Christian union—Case studies.
I. Ford, John T. II. Swan, Darlis J.

BX8.2.T94 1993

280'.042—dc20   93-4936

CIP

TWELVE TALES UNTOLD

Contents

CONTENTS

Contents

ECUMENICAL REFLECTIONS

Preface

Questions continue to abound about how the results of official dialogues between our churches are communicated to the "grassroots." Reception, the process whereby dialogue results are incorporated into the faith and life of the church, involves much more than publishing reports in the hope that somehow people in all expressions of the church will read them. First of all, there is a need for synthesis of the dialogue reports with other information about ecumenical work being done at the local level. Secondly, there is a need to make connections among the dialogue reports themselves.

Twelve Tales Untold is an attempt to answer both of these needs. Through the use of narratives from actual situations that have occurred in congregations and local communities, the authors have tried to draw on the multitude of consensus or convergence statements, demonstrating that these agreements do offer solutions. The narratives are organized around baptism, eucharist, and ministry in order to unify the issues arising from daily lives of Christians in a pluralistic society. For those who want to be further challenged, the authors have included several articles for theological reflection. That is not to say that the readers will not need to reflect on their own theologies as they try to answer the questions at the end of each narrative. In fact, there is where their theological foundations may be challenged and perhaps widened the most as they bring the theoretical to bear on the practical concerns.

Although there has been an attempt to bring unity to the concerns, the authors have not attempted uniformity. The case study model allows for people from various traditions — Episcopalian, Lutheran, Methodist, Orthodox, Pentecostal, Reformed, Roman Catholic, and others — to tell their stories in a unique way, depending on their different histories. The authors have tried to include a multicultural dimension and to be sensitive to issues of gender. While the target audience is those in local communities, the authors have included not only the questions from parishes and congregations but also from local councils of churches.

As questions of ecclesiology or the nature of church become more prevalent, one's "tradition" and how it is brought to bear on the telling of one's story may become even more significant. Perhaps more official dialogues will not appear on the horizon; but most certainly Christians will continue to be challenged to find more creative ways to "receive" what has already been accomplished. In this spirit of hope and expectation for the vitality of the Gospel message, we offer this study guide for ecumenical reception.

Introduction

MICHAEL ROGNESS

How has the ecumenical movement affected you? To what extent has it changed the way you relate to other Christians and groups in your own parish or congregation? Dialogues among theologians are an important aspect of the ecumenical movement, but formal theological dialogue involves relatively few of us. The purpose of this book is to consider the question, How has ecumenical activity been "received" on the local level?

This book will consider the reception of ecumenism among people in our churches by presenting twelve case studies. They are "twelve tales" based on actual situations, but the stories are "untold" because in some cases we do not know how they will end and in other cases there might have been different endings. These stories and other similar stories are not finished because ecumenism itself is still in progress. Readers may recognize similar situations in their own lives.

We chose the case study method of presenting ecumenical issues for four reasons:

1. Most people encounter ecumenism through everyday situations as members of different traditions deal with their

1

differences and work out agreements. A case study approach to the consideration of these issues will help readers see how ecumenism touches us in all kinds of situations.

2. Case studies inevitably draw us into theological discussion. Ecumenism is not a matter of the "scholarly level" in contrast to the "practical level." The questions we face are of one fabric. Practical situations reflect theological questions, and vice versa.

3. We hope these cases will help readers think ecumenically as other issues arise. There are dozens of such situations we might have examined, and we hope that by reading and discussing these cases, readers will learn to think and work ecumenically in other circumstances as well.

4. Ecumenism does not filter down from above. Much of the vigor of the ecumenical movement comes from local situations where people are striving together toward further unity. These case studies give a glimpse not only of ecumenical problems but also of the rich possibilities that open up as we live and work together.

We have organized these case studies around the three topics of the ecumenical study, *Baptism, Eucharist and Ministry* (BEM), prepared by the Faith and Order Commission of the World Council of Churches and approved in 1982. This seemed natural for us because many churches have already been involved in the study of BEM. These topics have also been studied in many of the bilateral conversations between church bodies. Furthermore, many of the ecumenical issues we face in congregations cluster around these same three topics. The introductory section of this book includes suggestions for the use of educational materials and a study guide for using cases.

The final section of this book includes a theological reflection on ecumenical reception, an essay on reception in the American situation, and an overview of reception at the local and regional levels. A bibliography is included for further study.

2

Introduction

An enormous amount of progress has been made toward increased understanding in ecumenical dialogues, but this work is only gradually becoming known by the people in our parishes. We hope that these chapters will draw readers into the discussion, so that ecumenism might sink its roots deep into our churches and help us realize the unity we have been given in Jesus Christ!

Use of Educational Materials

DARLIS J. SWAN

Church leaders at the "grassroots" have been asking for ways to explore the relationship between ecumenical dialogue at the national and international levels and the kind of practical ecumenism that takes place locally. These questions arise not only from pastors and professional church workers in parishes or congregations but also from those in local councils of churches. *Twelve Tales Untold* is designed to engage the two groups — those in national leadership and those leading in local situations — in a reciprocal relationship. The case study model, whose use is described in the next section, has been developed as a means of encouraging reception, the process whereby the results of ecumenical dialogue become part of the life and faith of our churches. This section on the use of educational materials describes the theory behind this method and suggests ways that it can be used to guide leaders in a variety of ecumenical settings. The term "learner" is used here to refer to anyone in a parish education program or other ecumenical setting where present views and attitudes are challenged and new information is acquired.

The writers of this volume have presupposed that once the education methodology has been established, an education

4

leader can make additional plans based on the proposed method, adapting it to his or her situation. For example, if a parish education leader assumes that a discussion of baptism is an appropriate starting point for a catechetical program, then he or she would start with a session on that topic, follow a study guide, and make plans to introduce images of baptism. The leader might ask the learners to recall their own baptisms or arrange for the class to attend a worship service that includes a baptism. In either case, the learners start with their own experience and then reflect on the implications of their experience. The point is that having a method in mind, the leader can use creativity and ingenuity to provide individual attention and stimulate learning.

As the writers designed this book, they operated from several premises that helped to determine their methodology. **The experience of the learner is always the appropriate starting point for a good educational program.** This is especially true in a study of reception, which has both classic and contemporary definitions. If reception is viewed as a dynamic process in which all expressions of the church participate, then it has relevance for all who have struggled with questions of religious identity. Once learners have focused on their experiences, they need to reflect upon them to test the significance of those events for their lives. In a sense, the reception of theological agreements calls for the community to test whether an agreement is representative of the positions held in the church and affirmed in the faith and life of the community. That includes the entire church and relates directly to parish life.[1]

By choosing case studies that deal with actual situations in which Christians have found themselves, the writers have tried not only to meet the needs of the learners but also to

---

1. See Richard Robert Osmer, *A Teachable Spirit: Recovering the Teaching Office in the Church* (Louisville, Ky.: Westminster/John Knox, 1990), for a contemporary proposal for interpreting centers of authority in the Protestant tradition. Note especially pp. 175–211.

challenge them with new information and images. This can lead them to question and perhaps to reinterpret what they have been taught about other Christian traditions. For example, the case studies relating to ministry introduce new issues and decisions that are confronting the churches today relating to such questions as, What is the role of the laity? What does it mean to be an inclusive church? What is the nature of ecumenical ministry? What kind of guidelines are required for ecumenical ministry? Several case studies describe the challenges involved at all levels when long-standing traditions of ministry are broken. Since the cases involve narratives taken directly from parish situations, most leaders and learners will find questions that directly touch their lives.

As far as the reflection part of the method is concerned, the questions that the learners are asked have been designed to draw them into not only the parish situation but also a study of theological agreements, such as *Baptism, Eucharist and Ministry* (BEM). The reflection process becomes twofold: (1) the learners interpret their own experience; (2) the learners see the relevance of theological agreements for their own faith journeys.

A sound religious education program includes both affective and cognitive domains. This premise follows the first one directly because it relates the experiential dimension, which is the core of the first premise, to other aspects of the learning process. The case study model, with its emphasis on images, has the potential for changing attitudes and beliefs. This model moves learning into the realm of affective education where thoughts and feelings are involved. Since affectivity is such an important aspect of religious experience, any program dealing with reception can make use of it. The narratives in this book have the potential to bring about a kind of "conversion," freeing the learners to examine other churches in the Christian tradition and to enter into dialogue with them.

If one is to approach the identity issues, which are integral to the reception process, then one might set goals to explore the *affective* dimensions of education. Stories, images, pic-

6

tures, and visions are inherent in any discussion of identity, and they are integral to one's own religious experience as well as to that of the community. Although there are many layers of meaning to be penetrated before core beliefs can be changed, approaching reception through story and myth is an effective way to begin. By using that starting point, an education leader can begin a process to change stereotypes and lead learners to embrace a larger and greater vision of Christian unity.

The *cognitive* domain is equally important in education for reception. One major reason why Christian churches have not moved further toward unity is that the reception process simply has not taken place within parishes and other local ecumenical settings. Not only are many Christians unaware of the many statements of convergence and even consensus that have been produced as a result of bilateral and multi-lateral dialogues, but many do not know that dialogues have occurred. While cooperative ecumenical projects abound in some localities, the theologies of the groups involved may never be explored.

Leaders in religious education at all levels of the churches as well as those who lead in other ecumenical settings have the responsibility of communicating and interpreting the results of ecumenical agreements to their constituencies. Although some of the agreements are tedious and laborious, study guides are available to assist in making them understandable for those who do not have the technical language that those documents presume. It is not enough just to share the documents. Information about these agreements must be disseminated. Those who have not participated in the official dialogues may also be interested in receiving information about them so that they can replicate the process in local settings. If that does not happen, those documents do not have the chance to be affirmed by the churches.

One shining star in this realm is BEM, a document that has touched irrevocably people who may have never seen its contents. In this book the writers have made references to

BEM where the case studies relate directly to its contents. Also, the leaders will find an annotated bibliography at the end of this book to assist them in focusing on the cognitive domain, in studying the actual documents from the dialogues, and in relating them to the particular case studies.

In order to ensure that the case studies really embody both affective and cognitive domains and can touch those who are willing to engage themselves in studying them, the members of the Reception Study Committee, who are primarily responsible for the writing of this volume, tested them. The "field testing," which involved discussing the cases as a study group, proved to be both educational and fun. It is the conviction of the Study Committee that the case studies can be the springboard for both *cognitive* and *affective* learning.

Ecumenical learning is most effective when it is done in the context of a total religious education program. Education for reception is best done in the context of the entire parish education program and other local ecumenical expressions. The case study model was designed with a wholistic approach centering on the worship experience as the main focus for all education in the community. Ecumenical education needs to permeate the life of the community rather than remain an isolated topic for a single adult forum or one Sunday church school session.

If the contents of this volume can be incorporated into the year's curriculum or discussion plan for groups — for example by interspersing interesting case studies according to themes — the learners will view it as essential to their education. Others may want to use this volume as a springboard for discussion. In either case, the return for the parish, local ecumenical groups, and perhaps the entire church will be greater if education for reception can be integrated.

Ecumenical education is itself part of the reception of ecumenical documents. Education for reception should be integrated into the parish education program just as the sacraments ought to be an integral part of catechetical programs. For example, in the Evangelical Lutheran Church in America, as well as in its predecessor church bodies, Luther's *Small Catechism* has served as the unifying principle and doctrinal foundation for all confirmation curriculum. In his *Small Catechism,* Martin Luther taught that the sacraments are essential for life in the Christian community, and every Christian ought to long to receive them and desire to understand their significance.

The present curriculum for confirmation in the Evangelical Lutheran Church in America begins with a study of baptism for several reasons: (1) confirmands have already experienced that sacrament and are prepared to discuss its meaning in their lives; (2) Luther's focus on the importance of Word and sacrament can be introduced; and (3) a discussion of baptism is an appropriate way to stress the death and resurrection of Jesus Christ as the core of the Christian community.

One reason why ecumenical learning and especially education for reception should not be allowed to exist in isolation is that religious education is primarily relational. Ecumenical education presupposes a holistic approach because *oikoumene* — "relating to the whole inhabited earth" — is suggestive of that thrust toward unity. While analysis may be necessary, ultimately learners seek a synthesis as a way of controlling their environment. In a contemporary world where "disconnects" abound not only in a technological sense but also in a behavioral context, leaders in religious education need to provide "connections" for all Christians. Unity in Christ is clearly the vital core and thread.

It is the hope of the Reception Study Committee that this volume will not exist in isolation but will become part of the mainstream of study materials for religious education in parishes and other communities concerned with Judeo-Christian values. The research of this particular writer indicates that when study guides relating to doctrine, particularly those emanating from the Lutheran bilateral dialogues in the United States, have been published as separate pieces, they have not been widely used and in some cases ignored.

One prime example of this from the Lutheran tradition is the elusive *Faith and Action* series published in the 1940s. That series included at least one piece that attempted to explain how Christian churches differ from one another in matters of doctrine. Although that item in the series would have little value for ecumenical education today, it serves to illustrate how learnings that are not integrated have only minuscule impact on the life and practice of the church.

Ecumenical education is best facilitated when information is organized according to themes. Good religious education programs are organized around a major principle to which all the information is related. In this volume the organizing principle is baptism, eucharist, and ministry. Although it is significant that these themes constitute the title of perhaps the most popular ecumenical convergence statement, they were not copied from it.

Common themes appear in the common or agreed statements of the multilateral and bilateral dialogues of the past twenty-five years. For instance, an examination of the Lutheran bilaterals in the United States indicates that the following themes important for Lutheran identity are present: (1) authority of Scripture, (2) creeds and documents, (3) ecclesiology, (4) sacraments, (5) ministry, (6) Gospel, and (7) justification and sanctification. These themes are important for Lutherans, but the dialogue process revealed that they were significant for the other dialogue partners, although each had a somewhat different way of stating their significance.

Lutherans believe that there are two sacraments, baptism and eucharist, as these have been instituted by Christ according to the biblical testimony. These "signs" of God's divine will and favor toward those who believe are recognized by the Lutheran ecumenical partners.[2] Such shared beliefs are

2. For information on Lutheran participation in ecumenical dialogues, see Joseph A. Burgess, ed., *Lutherans in Ecumenical Dialogue: A Reappraisal* (Minneapolis: Augsburg, 1990). See also William A. Novgren and William G. Rusch, eds., *"Toward Full Communion" and*

authenticated by what the partners said as they dialogued with Lutherans. These partners — Baptists, Episcopalians, evangelical conservatives, Methodists, Reformed, and Roman Catholics — attach great importance to baptism and eucharist. Roman Catholics add to the list holy orders, confirmation, marriage, penance, and anointing of the sick. Baptists prefer to call baptism and the Lord's Supper "ordinances," emphasizing Christ's command. The term "eucharist" was used primarily by Lutherans, Roman Catholics, and Episcopalians in the Lutheran bilateral, while others used "Lord's Supper." In those dialogues, Lutherans appeared to be comfortable using either term.

This volume on reception was written on the premise that certain themes, revealed in the dialogue process and elsewhere, are held dear by Christians in the American context who have participated in the ecumenical movement that took shape in the 1960s and gained momentum through the 1980s. The writers of this volume hope that those who study it will find it useful for organizing and reflecting on their ecumenical experiences and for fostering and encouraging new ones.

"*Concordat of Agreement*," Lutheran-Episcopal Dialogue, Series III (Minneapolis: Augsburg Fortress, 1991) and Keith F. Nickle and Timothy F. Lull, eds., *A Common Calling: The Witness of Our Reformation Churches in North American Today,* The Report of the Lutheran-Reformed Committee for Theological Conversations, 1988–1992 (Minneapolis: Augsburgh Fortress, 1993) as well as other bilateral reports.

A Study Guide for Using Cases

JOHN T. FORD

Case studies have long been used as educational tools in a number of professions. For example, legal instruction inevitably involves an extensive study of cases, since English common law is built upon a series of decisions in particular cases. Similarly, in schools of business administration, cases are often used as a means for training people in both economic theory and management techniques. Likewise, in the study of medicine, cases are widely used for instructional purposes.

Cases have also been widely used in theological education; for many years, cases were used to show ministerial students how to apply theological principles to practical pastoral situations. In the past, such training frequently took the form of casuistry, in which students were taught the "right response" to typical ethical questions. In such an approach, cases were used to illustrate the application of theological principles to particular situations.

In recent years, theological educators have emphasized the uniqueness of each pastoral situation and so have stressed the need for working out ethical decisions by bringing a given situation into dialogue with the appropriate theological principles. Instead of imposing a prefabricated solution on a "typical problem," pastors are taught to help people to see the theological issues involved in their problems, to consider possible solutions, to evaluate these possibilities in terms of their Christian commitment, and only then to make a decision.[1]

Cases, employed in this way, are at the intersection of theological theory and pastoral practice. When well used as teaching tools, cases demand that theories be tested by their practical applicability and that practice be evaluated by sound theory. A good case is not only one that tells an interesting story but also one that challenges people to look at the larger theological issues lurking behind the particular facts.

As pedagogical tools, case studies are intended to be instruments for facilitating reflection and discussion not only about the details of a particular case but also about the theological issues and spiritual values underlying that case. Such issues and values are not always immediately evident. Indeed what may be a vexing problem for one person may seem insignificant to another. For example, some see no reason why all baptized Christians should not be invited to share the eucharist whenever it is celebrated; others, however, insist that only members of their own church should be permitted to receive the eucharist. Case studies are one way of surfacing the different theological viewpoints that separate Christians.

Frequently, such divergent theological perspectives are incorporated into the ecclesiastical norms of different denominations; for example, a church that sees the eucharist as a sign of fellowship among all baptized Christians may officially invite everyone to communion, regardless of their denominational affiliation. In contrast, a church that sees the eucharist as the sign of the community that actually exists among its own members may refuse to admit people who are not members of

1. For examples of case studies designed for use in theological education, see Keith R. Bridston, et al., eds., *Casebook on Church and Society* (Nashville: Abingdon Press, 1974) and Robert A. and Alice F. Evans and Louis and Carolyn Weeks, *Casebook for Christian Living: Value Formation for Families and Congregations* (Atlanta: John Knox Press, 1977).

their church to the eucharist. While it is evident that different Christian churches have different regulations about the reception of the eucharist, the divergence in underlying theological reasons is not always immediately evident.

The following case studies have been prepared to uncover such basic theological issues. In one way or another, all these cases reveal some divergence, sometimes even conflict, between different theologies, ecclesiastical norms, and pastoral practices. Indeed, there would be "no real case" unless different theological views and values were somehow in conflict. However, such differences only parallel the legal world, where there would be no cases unless two parties were in conflict; or the business world, where there are different approaches to resolving economic problems; or the medical world, where there are different types of treatment for the same disease.

The cases presented here have both variety and complexity, but this is only a reflection of the diversity of American life in general and contemporary American Christianity in particular. These cases also have elements of divisiveness and ambiguity; on the contemporary scene, diversity often leads to divisiveness and plurality often offers ambiguous choices. Such tensions in modern life have their counterparts on the ecumenical scene. Christians frequently differ on what theological principles are applicable in a particular situation. But these cases also implicitly ask, Are there ecumenically acceptable solutions to these cases?

The most challenging cases are not those that are easily solved, but those that raise questions that need to be discussed. Thus a "good case" entails a search for alternatives in a particular situation. Unlike that type of casuistry that furnishes a standard response to all cases in a given category, the cases presented here allow for a number of possible solutions, a number of different scenarios. The difference in responses ultimately rests on the way in which one decides which theological principles are applicable in a given situation, as well as one's pastoral sensitivity in applying those principles in the actual situation.

Each of these cases is concerned with a significant ecumenical problem. This is not to say that the problems treated in these cases will occur again; rather, the problems presented are intended to raise basic ecumenical questions. Thus, the cases have been selected to illustrate particular ecumenical questions and so to serve as the basis for discussing broader ecumenical issues.

Each of these cases records an actual experience. A few of the cases are historical accounts, but in most cases the details have been disguised to protect the identity of those who shared their stories. All of these cases reveal some "crisis-point" in the life of an individual or in the life of a church. Common at a time of crisis is confusion about which way to go, about what options are available, about what decision to make. Some may be paralyzed by the unexpected challenge, others may opt for the traditional solutions of "the good old days," still others may search for more creative solutions.

The latter course is the one that the ecumenically minded must take. Instead of opting for the denominationally divided past, Christians today are challenged to seek an ecumenically united future. The way to that future, however, is far from clear, and so different people are pursuing different paths in the quest for unity. It should not be surprising then that in discussing these cases, different people will propose different alternatives or project different scenarios.

Obviously each of these cases had a specific ending, but the purpose in presenting these cases is not to encourage readers to second-guess that ending, as if reading a murder mystery. The reason for presenting each case is to challenge readers to reflect on what answers they might have given had they been in the same situation. Each case invites readers to become participants and to work out their own scenario — an ending that quite possibly might be more theologically justifiable, more pastorally appropriate, and more ecumenically creative than those that actually happened.

The cases do not have one "best ending." Consequently, different discussion groups might well formulate different "scenarios" for each of these cases. What is important is that the participants in such a discussion become ecumenically more sensitive through their dialogue about these cases.

There are a number of ways to start a discussion about these cases. An ecumenical discussion group may want to begin by encouraging each participant to ask, What would my church want me to do in this case? After hearing each participant's response, it might be beneficial for the group to discuss what the most ecumenically productive way of dealing with this situation might be. In some cases, a group may come to a consensus; in other cases, a group may find that it can only agree to disagree. In any event, it seems important for a group to ask, How could we provide an ecumenically satisfactory ending to this particular case?

Even if the discussion of cases does not lead to consensus, it should help all the participants acquire a greater sensitivity to ecumenical issues, as well as a greater appreciation of the faith and commitment of their partners in dialogue. The benefit of such a case study approach to ecumenism has been beautifully described by Elisabeth Schüssler Fiorenza:

> Case studies about the relations of women and men in society and church are theological reflections on very concrete experiences and ecclesial situations. Such a theological method is incarnational insofar as it does not begin with timeless ideas, principles or doctrines but seeks to discover divine presence and salvation in and through the communal, social-political life-praxis of the church, and to name it theologically. This method rests on an understanding of theology "as emerging from the interactions between what we make of the Christian story and tradition and what we make of contemporary life. It is at these points of interaction that God is to be encountered and discovered."[2]

2. "Liberation, Unity and Equality in Community: A New Testament Case Study," in *Beyond Unity-in-Tension: Unity, Renewal and the Community of Women and Men,* Faith and Order Paper 138, ed. Thomas F. Best (Geneva: WCC Publications, 1988), p. 58; the citation is from Mary Tanner, "Unity and Renewal: the Church and the Human Community," *The Ecumenical Review* 36 (1984): 254.

CASE STUDIES ON BAPTISM

1

Rebaptism of the Prodigal Son

(Lutheran/Baptist)

MICHAEL ROGNESS

An evangelistic team spent a month in Lakeville, holding a series of revival meetings attended by people of many denominations. A large number of youth attended, drawn particularly by the Christian rock music featured at the services.

Shortly after the group had left town, Russ, a college-age youth, visited Pastor Sprenger of Our Savior's Lutheran Church. He had never met Pastor Sprenger before, but he had been confirmed in that congregation by the previous pastor. Russ had been working in a nearby community for the past few years but had not been attending services at his home church.

Russ had attended the revival meetings and his faith had been reawakened. He asked Pastor Sprenger to rebaptize him because, as he put it, "Nothing happened when I was baptized as a baby, but now that I have accepted Jesus as my personal Savior, I want to be baptized again."

The pastor explained that Lutherans do not rebaptize people, even after a profoundly moving and life-changing experience. He talked about the reasons for infant baptism and explained why the church does not rebaptize. They parted on friendly terms.

Six months later, Russ returned to the pastor's office and explained that he had gone to a local Baptist church, where Pastor Taufer had baptized him. But he had not felt at home in that parish and now wished to renew his membership and activity in his former congregation. He asked Pastor Sprenger the following questions: (1) Did his rebaptism jeopardize his renewal of membership in his former parish? (2) If he were to rejoin the congregation, should he do something to "undo" his second baptism? (3) In the eyes of God, which was his "real" baptism? Had he offended God by being baptized again?

DISCUSSION QUESTIONS

In addition to Russ's own questions there are other issues that needed to be discussed. In this ecumenical age, where churches that practice "infant baptism" and churches that practice "believer's baptism" are seeking to understand each other better, how should churches relate to each other in pastoral situations such as these?[1]

1. Should the revival group have been aware that some people at their meetings had been baptized as infants? How should the revival group speak about baptism?

2. What should Pastor Sprenger have said when Russ asked for rebaptism?

3. How should Pastor Taufer have responded when Russ asked him for rebaptism?

4. Would it have been helpful for the two pastors to talk together,

---

1. "Baptism," par. 11 in *Baptism, Eucharist and Ministry,* points out that "Some churches baptize infants brought by parents or guardians who are ready, in and with the Church, to bring up the children in the Christian faith. Other churches practice exclusively the baptism of believers, who are able to make a personal confession of faith."

by themselves or with Russ? What might have been accomplished by such a conversation?

COMMENTARY

Baptism is universally recognized as the cornerstone of ecumenism. As the Second Vatican Council's 1964 Decree on Ecumenism states, "Baptism, therefore, constitutes a sacramental bond of unity linking all who have been reborn by means of it."[2]

After surveying the worldwide dialogues between Orthodox and Protestant church bodies, the World Council of Churches' Faith and Order Commission concluded, "The two partners recognize the validity of each other's rite of baptism if performed with water and in the name of the Trinity."[3]

More recently, *Baptism, Eucharist and Ministry* summarizes, "Our common baptism, which unites us to Christ in faith, is thus a basic bond of unity. We are one people and are called to confess and serve one Lord in each place and in all the world. The union with Christ which we share through baptism has important implications for Christian unity" (par. 6). Despite this recognition of baptism as a "bond of unity" among Christians and the nearly universal mutual recognition of baptism between various church bodies, "the real distinction is between those who baptize people at any age and those who baptize only those able to make a confession of faith for themselves" (commentary on par. 12).

This case study presents an actual situation (with names changed), dealing with the nature and age of baptism, the difference between "infant" and "believer's" baptism and the possibility or impossibility of mutual recognition by two

---

2. Decree on Ecumenism (22) in *The Documents of Vatican II*, ed. Walter M. Abbott, S.J. (New York: The Guild Press, 1966), p. 364.

3. Faith and Order Paper 76 (Geneva: World Council of Churches, 1975), p. 38.

churches. It is not at all a unique situation, but one that arises frequently, particularly in the United States, where baptismal practices vary widely.

Baptism, Eucharist and Ministry confronts this division in baptismal understanding and practice head-on by laying a foundation for a common understanding of baptism. Basic areas of agreement are outlined (par. 1–23). The document also concedes, "The inability of the churches mutually to recognize their various practices of baptism as sharing in the one baptism and their actual dividedness in spite of mutual baptismal recognition, have given dramatic visibility to the broken witness of the Church" (commentary on par. 6).

Baptism, Eucharist and Ministry acknowledges that for all churches "baptism is an unrepeatable act," that is, no church rebaptizes when the previous baptism in another church is recognized as valid. (Indeed, baptism is also unrepeatable for those who practice "believer's baptism." It is not a "re"-baptism, since infant baptism is not recognized as a valid baptism.) The document urges that "any practice which might be interpreted as 're-baptism' be avoided" (par. 13). It is clearly the view of those who wrote the document that rebaptism is a barrier to church unity that must be overcome:

> Churches which have insisted on a particular form of baptism or which have had serious questions about the authenticity of other churches' sacraments and ministries have at times required persons coming from other church traditions to be baptized before being received into full communicant membership. As the churches come to fuller mutual understanding and acceptance of one another and enter into closer relationships in witness and service, they will want to refrain from any practice which might call into question the sacramental integrity of other churches or which might diminish the unrepeatability of the sacrament of baptism. (Commentary on par. 13)

Because the topic of this volume is reception of new ecumenical agreements and relationships by churches, one must ask, Is it possible for those churches that practice "believer's baptism" to recognize the baptism of those baptized as infants?

When the Lutheran World Federation summarized the responses to *Baptism, Eucharist and Ministry* from Lutheran churches around the world, it expressed a hope for such recognition: "What is expected of the churches which practice adult baptism is the recognition of the Lutheran churches' own baptismal practice as a possible form of Christian baptism."[4] Is this expectation realistic? Baptist pastors and congregations might be on congenial terms with neighboring congregations, but can they recognize infant baptism of other Christians while retaining their own theological integrity? Are they not theologically compelled to rebaptize persons joining their churches who were baptized as infants? What further developments will be necessary before such mutual recognition can be achieved?

One might look to the example of Covenant churches, where the age of baptism is optional. Both kinds of baptism are practiced, with the choice left largely to the families involved. (Indeed, baptism itself is optional, although in most Covenant congregations believing Christians are strongly urged to be baptized.) However, the Covenant practice is deeply rooted in their history, and it presupposes an ambiguous understanding of baptism, which is unlikely to furnish a pattern for other churches.

---

4. Michael Seils, ed. *Lutheran Convergence? An Analysis of the Lutheran Responses to Baptism, Eucharist and Ministry,* Lutheran World Federation Report 25 (Geneva: Lutheran World Federation, 1988), p. 47.

POSSIBLE OUTCOMES

1. Rebaptism by the Lutheran pastor is not a possibility. *Baptism, Eucharist and Ministry* acknowledges baptism as an "unrepeatable act," a statement that met with widespread, worldwide agreement among Lutheran churches and is a conviction shared by other churches practicing infant baptism.[5]

However, a few months earlier, Pastor Sprenger had consulted with a woman who had been increasingly disturbed after learning that her baptismal records had been destroyed in a church fire. Furthermore, no family members were alive who might have witnessed her baptism. In that instance Pastor Sprenger had baptized her *conditionally* — a "conditional" provision recognized by his church body.

2. If Pastor Taufer was under the impression that Russ had indeed rejected the validity of his infant baptism, one would expect him to rebaptize such a person. Rebaptism has been the traditional policy of Baptist churches, and it is consistent with their theology. However, if Pastor Taufer knew that Russ's intent was not to join the Baptist church but to return to his home congregation, would he still have baptized him?

3. Imagine this situation between church groups, both practicing infant baptism, and pose the questions, Are there instances when a pastor or priest would rebaptize? Under what circumstances would a pastor or priest say, "Your previous baptism is not valid, so I shall baptize you here and now"?

Baptism, Eucharist and Ministry hopes that "wherever possible, mutual recognition should be expressed explicitly by the churches" (par. 15). Such a recovery of baptismal unity is "at the heart of the ecumenical task as it is central for the

---

5. Seils, *Lutheran Convergence?* p. 46.

realization of genuine partnership within the Christian communities" (commentary on par. 6).

One avenue toward such recognition is that the two sides learn from each other. Those who practice believer's baptism "may seek to express more visibly the fact that children are placed under the protection of God's grace," and those who practice infant baptism "must guard themselves against the practice of apparently indiscriminate baptism and take more seriously their responsibility for the nurture of baptized children to mature commitment to Christ" (par. 16).

2

Mestizaje: A Mixing of Cultures and Churches

(Roman Catholic/Christian)

JOHN T. FORD

"Not only is a picture worth a thousand words, but this one explains the past three months of my ministry." So thought Joe Smith as he stared with a mixture of fascination and frustration at the front-page picture in *El Latino*, the city's Spanish weekly.

As a first-year seminary student, Joe had felt lucky to land a part-time placement at Central City Church. A Spanish major in college, Joe had spent a year in Spain as an exchange student. When the church advertised for a student minister to start a program in Hispanic ministry in the neighborhood where the church was located, Joe's fluency in Spanish and commitment to the project had so impressed the ministry committee that it was willing to take the risk of hiring a first-year student.

The ministry committee was also impressed with Joe's proposed strategy of beginning this new ministry with a combination of Bible study and English lessons. Joe prepared a flyer that announced the formation of a Bible study group that would be followed by an English class; both would meet at the church on Wednesday evenings. Then with the assistance of the church's two Hispanic employees, Joe personally distributed the announcements to Hispanics who lived in the apartment buildings near the church.

Attendance on the first Wednesday was modest enough: the two Hispanic employees came with their spouses and three of their friends. However, the Bible study went well and Joe's bilingual ability made the English classes a huge success. At the end of class, Joe thanked each person for attending and invited each one to bring a friend the following week.

During the coming week, Joe was a bit nervous whether anyone would show up. However, he needn't have worried: fifteen people came, the Bible study about baptism occasioned a lively discussion, and at the end of the English class everyone joined in saying the Lord's prayer in English. As he said "adios," one of the young men asked Joe if he could bring his guitar the next time. Joe encouraged him to do so.

The next Wednesday, two dozen people attended. The Bible study concluded with several lively hymns in Spanish and at the end of English class, Joe fingered out a simple hymn on the piano, which the guitarist quickly picked up; and the class started learning a hymn in English.

By the end of October, weekly attendance reached forty and Joe suggested that it might be well to start a second session on Monday nights. He hoped that would be a way of dividing the English class into two more manageable groups of twenty each. He told people that they could come Monday or Wednesday or both.

The next week when there were two sessions, Joe was pleasantly surprised that forty-some people came on Monday and over fifty came on Wednesday — though many of these were repeaters, who didn't seem to mind repeating the same Bible study and English class. In addition, the guitarist had recruited a half-dozen friends to form a music group, Los Renacidos (The Born Again), who played both nights.

In November, when Joe had his regular monthly meeting with the ministry committee, its members were extremely pleased with the growth of Joe's ministry. One committee member asked whether those in the Hispanic program would like to attend the regular Sunday services. Joe replied that he suspected that most of them would not feel at home at an "Anglo" service, but that he would invite them. Another committee member asked whether the church should start a Sunday service in Spanish. Joe replied that he had already asked the Bible study groups whether they would like to have a worship service together on Sunday, but everyone seemed to prefer the evening meetings, though he wasn't quite sure why.

Joe then inquired whether the ministry committee would be willing to invite Los Renacidos to play at the regular service in a couple weeks. The committee agreed that this would be a good way to show the Hispanics that they were welcome at Sunday services. However, when Joe later asked the music group whether they would play at services on the second Sunday of December, they replied that they were already *muy ocupados.*

Joe was a bit puzzled at their refusal; in the past, they had always been eager to play. However, he knew that many Hispanics had to work on Sunday.

The full-color picture in *El Latino* provided the explanation. The feature story described the fiesta of Our Lady of Guadalupe at Capilla Latina, the nearby Roman Catholic church. Front and center in the picture were Los Renacidos.

Joe felt hurt that the group had turned down his request but then played at another church. He decided to see what would happen the following Monday. Los Renacidos were there in full strength, as enthusiastic as ever. After class, Joe simply could not keep himself from showing them their picture and asking them to which church they belonged.

After some moments of hesitation, one of the group asked, "Do we have to choose? We like to come here to study the Bible, but we also love Guadalupe; we sing one set of songs when we come here; we sing other songs when we go to Capilla Latina. We like both. After all, we are people who must live in two worlds; we have to live in two different cultures. So why shouldn't we go to two different churches?"

Joe was at a loss for words. One of the group then asked, *"Hasta miércoles?"* ("See you on Wednesday?") Joe managed to reply, *"Por supuesto, hasta entonces"* ("Of course, see you then"). Each of the Los Renacidos then gave Joe an *abrazo* (a hug) and left. Joe spent most of the intervening hours wondering whether the group really would come back.

True to their word, Los Renacidos were all back on Wednesday, as eager as ever to discuss the Bible and play their music. Joe was relieved to see them; the Bible study and English class went on with the usual enthusiasm. But Joe wondered how he was going to explain this development to the ministry committee.

When Joe met with the committee, the reactions ranged from anger to amusement. One member felt that the time had come for a choice: "They've got to choose between Central City Church and Capilla Latina." Another member remarked that maybe it was unrealistic to expect Anglos and Hispanics to attend the same service. A third member commented, "God may be telling us something — maybe this is a good opportunity for ecumenical cooperation." The ministry committee eventually, but somewhat reluctantly, decided that since it had given Joe a free hand in developing this ministry, he should have similar freedom in handling the situation. Joe left the meeting wondering what he should do.

Back at the seminary, Joe scheduled a meeting with his pastoral supervisor. Joe asked whether he should make the group choose between Central City Church and Capilla Latina.

"If you did that, what choice would they make?" his supervisor asked. Joe realized that by forcing a choice, he might be ending his ministry. Then Joe asked whether he should start a Sunday service in Spanish.

"Do they want such a service?"

Joe had to admit that the group probably preferred to go to Capilla Latina on Sunday.

The supervisor then commented, "Yet the people obviously like your Bible study and English classes."

When Joe agreed, his supervisor added, "In other words, going to two churches isn't their problem, it's your problem!"

Joe acknowledged that such might be the case. Then his supervisor asked, "Is your ministry only for those who are members of Central City Church?"[1]

Joe was relieved that he had to go to class and he could end the conversation there.

The following day, Joe made an appointment with his theology professor to pursue the question of church membership.

His professor asked, "How does a person become a member of the church?"

"I guess by having his or her name entered on the church register," Joe replied.

"How did you become a member of the church?" asked his professor.

Joe answered, "My parents did it for me, since I was baptized as an infant."

The professor smiled. "Then baptism is basically what makes a person a member of the church?"

Joe stuttered, "Well, I'd still like to have people registered."

His professor continued, "Do you think that the people who are coming to your Bible study classes are members of the church?"

Joe then recalled that during the Bible study about baptism, all those in the group had told him that they had been baptized, most of them like him as infants.

The professor then asked, "If any of them decided to join Central City Church, would you rebaptize them?" When Joe hesitated, his professor added, "Were you rebaptized when you started your ministry at Central City?"

1. See the statement of the World Council of Churches on "Christian Witness, Proselytism, and Religious Liberty" (1960), which can be found in *A Documentary History of the Faith and Order Movement 1927-1963,* ed. Lukas Vischer (St. Louis: Bethany Press, 1963), pp. 183-196.

"Of course not," Joe answered.

"Then why rebaptize others?" Joe didn't have an answer.

Then his professor asked, "If these people are baptized, aren't they already members of the Church? Notice I said members of the Church, not necessarily of Central City Church."

Joe wasn't sure what to say next, but his professor saved him the trouble by giving him a booklet on *Baptism, Eucharist and Ministry*.[2]

"Why don't you read what this says about baptism and then come back and we can continue our discussion next week?"

A few days later, Joe happened to attend an all-day conference with students from other seminaries. Also attending was Juan Diego, a Mexican-American Roman Catholic. At lunch, the two began chatting in Spanish. Joe decided to tell Juan about his ministry with Hispanics. When Juan heard about Los Renacidos coming to Bible study at Central City Church yet celebrating the fiesta of Guadalupe at Capilla Latina, he began laughing.

"Please don't be offended by my laughing, but I would have done the same."

When Joe said that he was more puzzled than ever, Juan replied, "You speak Spanish very well, indeed your grammar and vocabulary are better than mine and I have been speaking Spanish all my life. But you need to understand that I and many other Hispanics are *mestizos* — people of mixed blood, people of a mixture of cultures. My parents were born in Mexico, but I was born in the United States; yet I have many Mexican relatives whom I love to visit. South of what we Mexicans call the Río Bravo, I am Mexican; north of what we Americans call the Rio Grande, I am American."

---

2. This document, which has been published in many places, can be found in Harding Meyer and Lukas Vischer, eds., *Growth in Agreement: Reports and Agreed Statements of Ecumenical Conversations on a World Level* (New York: Paulist Press; Geneva: World Council of Churches, 1984), pp. 465–503.

Joe had to laugh. "I think I get what you're telling me; I guess if one river can have two names, then a Christian might be able to have two churches."

Juan smiled. "I'm not sure how good that conclusion is theologically, since, like you, I'm a first year student, but at least it may help you understand why we *mestizos* — who are used to moving back and forth across the border from one culture to another, sometimes speaking one language and other times speaking the other language — may not find anything unusual about going to two different churches."[3]

The conference day came to an end and it was time for Joe and Juan to return to their respective seminaries. Joe asked Juan if he would like to come to Bible study one evening next week. Juan replied, "Of course, but then will you come with me to Capilla Latina?"

DISCUSSION QUESTIONS

1. If you were Joe, would you continue to conduct the Bible study group and English classes?

2. If you were Joe, how would you explain your decision to the

3. For an introduction to Hispanic ministry, perhaps the best available work (with particular emphasis on the Mexican-American experience) is Allan Figueroa Deck, *The Second Wave: Hispanic Ministry and the Evangelization of Cultures* (New York: Paulist Press, 1989). A short history that records the discrimination experienced by Hispanics in the United States and in North American churches is Moises Sandoval, *On the Move: A History of the Hispanic Church in the United States* (Maryknoll, N.Y.: Orbis, 1990). To date, the main theological interpreter of the Mexican-American religious experience is Virgilio Elizondo; a short autobiographical introduction is *The Future is Mestizo: Life Where Cultures Meet* (Bloomington, Ind.: Meyer-Stone Books, 1988); longer treatments are provided by Elizondo in *Galilean Journey: The Mexican-American Promise* (Maryknoll, N.Y.: Orbis, 1985) and *Christianity and Culture: An Introduction to Pastoral Theology and Ministry for the Bicultural Community* (San Antonio: Mexican-American Cultural Center, 1975).

ministry committee? To your pastoral supervisor? To your theology professor?

3. What is your view of the mission of the Church? Is it to serve others? To preach the Gospel? To have people participate in Sunday services? To gain new members? To preserve the century-long tradition of Central City Church in a changing neighborhood?

4. What is your attitude toward "proselytizing" (asking members of another church to join your church)?

5. Is it possible to be a member of more than one church?

6. If you were Joe and Juan came to your Bible study group, would you then join him at Capilla Latina?

7. If you were Juan, would you go to Joe's Bible study and invite him to Capilla Latina?

3

A Paschal Night

(Greek Orthodox/Roman Catholic)

PATRICK VISCUSO

It had been a long Holy Week at Holy Trinity Greek Orthodox Church. Father Nick Papakosta was exhausted. Nevertheless, Great Saturday night was a moving spiritual experience for the priest. At midnight in the midst of the darkened church, the beckoning light shown from the altar as Father Nick chanted, *"Devte lavete phos . . ."* ("Come receive the light"), a hymn that resounded throughout the church as members of the congregation lighted their own candles. Father Nick proclaimed, *"Christos anesti"* ("Christ is risen"), and all responded, *"Alethos anesti"* ("He has truly risen"). With the bells ringing, the Divine Liturgy followed the Resurrection Matins.

Joining in this celebration of the ageless mystery of Easter were the members of the Poulos family. George, the head of the family, was by far the wealthiest member of Holy Trinity. Devoted both to his Orthodox faith and his Greek heritage, George had raised his only son, Christopher, in the Hellenic Tradition. Christopher had not only been taught Greek, he had even spent several summers with relatives in Athens. It was not surprising then that George Poulos as president of the church's board of trustees had publicly criticized every

34

attempt by Father Nick to introduce English into the services of the parish.

Christopher's Greek ancestry and training, however, had not deterred him from marrying Bridget O'Neill in the Roman Catholic Church. Subsequently, their three children, Christopher Jr., Meghan, and Sean, were baptized in the Roman Catholic Church. Father Nick saw Christopher and his family from time to time, since they always attended local Greek festivals. Although regretting that Christopher had chosen to marry and to educate his children in the Roman Catholic Church, Father Nick felt that at least there was one less Poulos to worry about.

As Father Nick glanced down the line of those approaching the altar for communion, his heart froze. Approaching the altar were Christopher Poulos and his three children. When Christopher reached the priest, he said, "My children's names are Christopher, Meghan, and Sean."

Father Nick responded softly but firmly, "I'm sorry, but none of you can receive communion. You were married outside the Greek Orthodox Church, and your children were baptized in the Roman Catholic Church."

Christopher replied, "Father, we're as Greek as anyone in this parish. Our name is Poulos and it is Easter."

Father Nick gently responded, "I'm sorry, Christopher, but the church is not an ethnic group. Since you were not married in the Orthodox Church, I am not allowed to give you communion. And since your children have never received chrismation, I am not allowed to give them communion."

Christopher insisted, "Look, Father, you're embarrassing me in front of my family and the entire Greek community." Christopher then raised his voice. "Either you give us communion or you're going to have a problem."

Father Nick replaced the red communion cloth over the chalice. "Christopher, anger is inappropriate for Easter. The most that I can do is to allow you and your children to kiss the chalice."

Glaring at the priest, Christopher escorted the three children down the main aisle and out of the church. As murmurs spread through the congregation, Christopher and his children were quickly followed out of the church by his father George and other Poulos relatives.

Father Nick had difficulty in concentrating and praying during the rest of the service. As he slowly folded his vestments after the service, he thought about the possible repercussions of this Paschal Night. Usually after a long Lenten fast and the lengthy Holy Week services, Father Nick looked forward to the traditional Easter dinner with his family. Instead he was worried about possible controversy and infighting within his congregation.

After a less-than-pleasant Easter, Father Nick decided to contact Christopher Poulos. He spent most of the following week unsuccessfully trying to reach Christopher. Father Nick's repeated calls went unreturned. The following Sunday, after liturgy, a relative of George Poulos asked, "Why wouldn't you give communion to Christopher and his children on Easter?"

When Father Nick replied that communion could only be given to those married and baptized in the Orthodox Church, the relative said, "Well, Father Prokopios gave all of them communion at St. Demetrios."

Father Nick couldn't believe what he heard. He immediately telephoned Father Prokopios Sophokleos, the pastor of St. Demetrios. "How could you allow Christopher Poulos to receive communion? He was married outside the Orthodox Church! And how could you give communion to his children? They were baptized Roman Catholics, not Greek Orthodox!"

Father Prokopios gently replied, "Nick, you and I marry Orthodox to Catholics, so why not share the bread of life with them?" Father Nick responded with restraint, "You have no right to act on your own and give the sacraments to non-Orthodox. The three children have never been chrismated!"

Father Prokopios replied condescendingly, "How can a priest deny communion to three children? They could be permanently alienated from the church."

Father Nick retorted, "Father Prokopios, you have no

right to act on your own and share the eucharist with non-Orthodox. The unity of faith must always precede the sharing of communion. Have you become protestantized? You've not only played fast and loose with the church's teachings, but you've also totally undercut my position in my parish!"

Father Nick abruptly ended the conversation. Yet he wondered why Father Prokopios had given communion to Christopher and his children. Surely Prokopios had some theological rationale; after all, he had obtained a doctorate in pastoral theology at a local Protestant seminary and prided himself on his knowledge of contemporary American theology.

In any case, Father Nick realized that the problem was his. He knew he must act and act soon; otherwise, both he and his congregation would be in turmoil. He wanted to be faithful to the Orthodox tradition as well as sensitive to the pastoral needs of his parishioners, particularly people like Christopher Poulos.

If you were Father Nick what would you do?

POSSIBLE OUTCOMES

1. Father Nick decided to follow the archdiocese's canonical regulations on marriage, baptism, and the eucharist. Along with many famous Orthodox canonists, he believed that Roman Catholics are baptized; however, their faith is not Orthodox. For Roman Catholics to receive communion, they must convert and be received through chrismation. On the following Sunday, he placed a notice in the parish bulletin: "The word 'communion' contains the word 'union.' We in the Greek Orthodox Church regard the reception of the eucharist as a manifestation of a person's union with the Orthodox Church, not as a means to unity. Consequently, we cannot give communion to those who have been married in other churches nor to those who have not converted to the Orthodox faith."

Later that week, Father Nick received a letter from George Poulos stating that he was resigning from the parish's board of trustees. Father Nick would not miss George, but he knew the parish could barely manage without George's sizeable donations.

2. Father Nick decided to follow the archdiocese's canonical practices, but believed that by the principle of "economy" the Greek Orthodox Church makes valid what is really invalid. Father Nick believed that Roman Catholic baptism is only an empty form, but that the Orthodox Church fills this form with grace when Roman Catholics convert and are received by chrismation.

At a local ecumenical meeting, Father Nick presented his view that the sacraments administered outside the Orthodox Church are false. The next issue of the city's newspaper headlined its report on his talk: "Father Nicholas Papakosta Hammers Heresy."

A few weeks later, when he attended a meeting of the local council of churches, he couldn't miss hearing the stage whispers: "Watch what you say, the Hammer of Orthodoxy is here."

3. Father Nick decided that Prokopios had the right idea. He called George Poulos: "On Easter, I made a terrible mistake in refusing communion to your son and grandchildren. I should have done as Father Prokopios did."

Father Nick explained to his parishioners that matrimony and baptism are pastoral sacraments that should be used in the spirit of "economy," a spirit of love. Many Greek Orthodox who had married Protestants, Roman Catholics, and non-Christians outside the Orthodox Church came to communion in both parishes. As a result, a number of Orthodox priests in the area found themselves in difficulty with their congregations and began to complain about what Father Nick and Father Prokopios were doing.

Father Nick chose to ignore these complaints until he received a letter from the bishop summoning him to a spiritual court to explain his actions. Father Prokopios telephoned Father Nick to say that he had received a similar letter.

4. Father Nick decided to do nothing. The Sunday after Easter, attendance was down — perhaps not too unusual in

comparison to the overflow crowd at Easter. However, the low attendance continued throughout the summer and into the fall. Father Nick realized that without the Poulos family and their friends, the parish could not continue financially. He reluctantly made an appointment with the bishop to request a new assignment.

DISCUSSION QUESTIONS

1. Should Christopher Poulos and Bridget O'Neill have been married in the Greek Orthodox Church?

2. In the eyes of the Greek Orthodox Church, were Christopher Jr., Meghan, and Sean validly baptized?

3. Why should Christopher Jr., Meghan, and Sean receive chrismation?

COMMENTARY

1. Marriages of Orthodox and Non-Orthodox

The Greek Orthodox Archdiocese allows the marriage of baptized Protestants and Roman Catholics with Orthodox if (a) the celebration takes place in the Orthodox Church, (b) the Orthodox priest is the sole celebrant, and (c) every effort is made afterward to raise any offspring as Orthodox.[1]

A non-Orthodox spouse is not required to convert if "baptized in the name of the Holy Trinity."[2] Marriages with non-Christians are strictly forbidden:

1. Robert G. Stephanopoulos, *Guidelines for Orthodox Christians in Ecumenical Relations* (New York: Standing Conference of Canonical Orthodox Bishops in America, 1973), pp. 19–22.
2. The Greek Orthodox Archdiocese of North and South America, *The Priest's Handbook* (Brookline: Holy Cross Press, 1978), p. 89.

A marriage cannot be blessed or recognized by the Orthodox Church between an Orthodox Christian and someone not of the Christian faith. Religious groups which are not of the Christian tradition include: adherents of Judaism and Islam; Buddhism, Hinduism and other Far Eastern religions or movements, the Mormons ("Latter-Day Saints"), Christian Scientists, Seventh-Day Adventists, Jehovah's Witnesses, and various cults.[3]

According to the official position of the Greek Orthodox Church, the priest is the minister of the sacrament of matrimony and a Greek Orthodox who marries in the Roman Catholic Church is excommunicated. Thus, Christopher would not be allowed to receive communion until he is reconciled by being married in the Orthodox Church. Bridget, however, would not be required to convert to the Orthodox faith.

Their situation might not have arisen had they been aware of the *Agreed Statement on Mixed Marriages* formulated by the Orthodox-Roman Catholic Consultation in the United States:

According to the view of the Orthodox Church the marriage of an Orthodox can only be performed by an Orthodox priest as the minister of the sacrament. In the view of the Catholic Church the contracting partners are the ministers of the sacrament, and the required presence of a Catholic major cleric as witness of the Church can be dispensed with for weighty reasons. In view of this, we recommend that the Catholic Church, as a normative practice, allow the Catholic party of a proposed marriage with an Orthodox to be married with the Orthodox priest officiating.[4]

---

3. *Marriage in the Greek Orthodox Church, Policy and Guidelines* (New York: The Greek Orthodox Archdiocese of North and South America, National Department of Church and Family Life), pp. 6–7.

4. "An Agreed Statement on Mixed Marriages" (20 May 1970),

2. *Greek Orthodox Recognition of Baptism*

The present practice of allowing the marriage of Orthodox with other baptized Christians without the requirement of conversion appears to imply that their baptism is recognized. This policy reflects decisions taken by the Patriarchal Synod of Constantinople at the end of the nineteenth century that Roman Catholic and Protestant converts already baptized in the name of the Trinity should be received by chrismation. Other converts should be baptized in the Orthodox Church.[5]

How should this policy be understood? Some Orthodox theologians understand the administration of chrismation to a person baptized in the name of the Trinity as an instance of "economy," a supplying of grace by the Church to the empty forms of Western baptism.[6] Other Orthodox theologians believe that the one baptism of the Church can be administered outside the boundaries of the Orthodox Church.

In the nineteenth century, the Patriarchal Synod of Constantinople decided that two methods of "economy" could be utilized in the case of marriages of an Orthodox with a baptized non-Orthodox: the chrismation of the non-Orthodox before the wedding, or a promise by both parties to raise all children in the Orthodox Church. The present practice of administering the sacrament of matrimony when one spouse is not Orthodox also appears to be a use of "economy" made in view of the good of the Church and the salvation of souls.

However, the reception of the eucharist is allowed only

---

in *Building Unity: Ecumenical Dialogues with Roman Catholic Participation in the United States,* ed. Joseph A. Burgess and Brother Jeffrey Gros, F.S.C. (New York: Paulist Press, 1989), p. 327.

5. For current policy, see Robert G. Stephanopoulos, *op. cit.,* pp. 18–19.

6. For an explanation of "economy," see "The Principle of Economy: A Joint Statement" (19 May 1976) in *Building Unity,* pp. 332–334; also, John H. Erickson, "*Oikonomia* in Byzantine Canon Law," in *Law, Church and Society,* ed. Kenneth Pennington and Robert Somerville (University of Pennsylvania Press, 1977), pp. 225–236.

for Orthodox, since communion is regarded as a sign of the unity of the faith. Thus, non-Orthodox spouses are not permitted to receive communion.

3. Greek Orthodox View of Chrismation

In the Orthodox Church, baptism is always celebrated in conjunction with chrismation and the reception of the eucharist. These three sacraments are customarily administered to infants, to those who have never been baptized, and to those whose baptisms are not recognized by the Orthodox Church.

Converts whose baptisms are recognized by the Greek Orthodox Church are customarily received by the administration of chrismation and then admitted to the reception of the eucharist. Thus, in the case of the Poulos children, in order to be admitted to communion, they should first receive chrismation.

4

Spirit Baptism

(Baptist/Pentecostal)

ROGER OLSON

A young woman named Agnes Ozman received the baptism of the Holy Spirit and spoke in tongues at Pastor Chuck Parham's First Pentecostal Assembly. Although she had been raised, converted, and baptized in water at First Baptist Church in the same city, Agnes felt something was lacking in her spiritual life. A friend invited her to a special service at the Pentecostal church and she attended, somewhat reluctantly. Agnes had always heard that Pentecostals were fanatical and certainly more emotional than Baptists. But she was surprised at the overwhelming love and acceptance she felt at this "full gospel" church, and at the end of a very enthusiastic gospel message by Pastor Parham she went forward to kneel at the altar. People gathered around her and laid hands on her head and shoulders and prayed for her to be filled with the Holy Spirit. In a sudden rush of ecstasy Agnes spoke in a strange language, and the Pentecostal people assured her that she had for the first time received the full baptism of the Holy Spirit.

Agnes basked in the glow of her new experience for days. She felt a new love for God and a desire for Christian growth and service. After thinking about where she could best serve

God, she went back to her home church, First Baptist, and spoke with her pastor. Pastor Williamson was not pleased to hear about her Pentecostal experience. He tried to be as receptive and supportive as possible, but when Agnes shared what had happened to her, he was dismayed. He reminded her that as a child she had to come forward after a Sunday evening service to accept Christ and then was baptized in water several Sunday nights later. "Didn't you receive the Holy Spirit then?" he asked Agnes. "Pastor, I really don't know. I don't remember feeling anything special, at least not like the experience I had at First Pentecostal Assembly. I think I was saved here at First Baptist Church. But I wasn't Spirit-filled until I attended Pastor Parham's church. Isn't that what happened to the disciples on the day of Pentecost? Weren't they already converted to Christ but only then received the baptism of the Holy Spirit?"

Pastor Williamson tried to explain that the day of Pentecost was the once-for-all outpouring of the Holy Spirit on the church and that every truly converted Christian after that is baptized in the Holy Spirit at the moment she is "born again." Water baptism is the sign and symbol of that Spirit baptism at conversion.

Agnes left her home church puzzled and confused. Where did she belong? What had really happened to her at First Pentecostal Assembly?

DISCUSSION QUESTIONS

Baptists and Pentecostals have very similar beliefs about most aspects of Christianity. However, they disagree strongly about the "subsequence" of the baptism of the Holy Spirit (whether it is a separate and subsequent experience to conversion/regeneration) and about glossolalia (speaking in tongues) as the "initial physical evidence" of Spirit baptism. Baptists traditionally deny both subsequence and evidential glossolalia.

The case of Agnes Ozman raises some questions for Baptist-Pentecostal dialogue and understanding:

1. Is there a way to reconcile Baptist and Pentecostal beliefs about Christian initiation and the role of the Holy Spirit in the life of the Christian? Is there a position that can bridge the gap between these two interpretations?

2. How could the Pentecostals of Pastor Parham's church have helped Agnes understand her renewing experience of the Holy Spirit without leading her to question her earlier experience?

3. Could Pastor Williamson have affirmed Agnes's Pentecostal experience without sacrificing basic Baptist belief about being filled with the Holy Spirit at conversion?

4. To what extent should Agnes trust her feelings about the role of the Holy Spirit?

COMMENTARY

A serious rift has developed between two branches of evangelical Christianity during the twentieth century. During the first decades of this century a large number of evangelicals began to interpret the revivals that happened among them (e.g., the famous "Azusa Street revival" in Los Angeles in 1906) as a fresh outpouring of the Holy Spirit. Building on earlier revivalists' teaching about a "second blessing" experience, these Pentecostals institutionalized belief in a "second definite work of grace" *subsequent* to conversion called the baptism of (in, with) the Holy Spirit and *added* a new twist — the experience of glossolalia as its necessary evidence.

Most evangelicals, including nearly all Baptists, hold that one aspect of Christian conversion is the baptism of the Holy Spirit. In this they agree with the main body of Protestant theology going back to Luther, Calvin, and Zwingli.[1]

1. For an in-depth analysis of the roots and development of Pente-

The world ecumenical movement seems to endorse the same view held by the Baptists — that baptism of the Holy Spirit is identical with Christian initiation. *Baptism, Eucharist and Ministry* states that "the paschal mystery of Christ's death and resurrection is inseparably linked with the pentecostal gift of the Holy Spirit. Similarly, participation in Christ's death and resurrection is inseparably linked with the receiving of the Spirit. Baptism in its full meaning signifies and effects both. . . . All agree that Christian baptism is in water and the Holy Spirit."[2]

However, this paragraph of BEM, taken in its entirety, may leave room for a modified form of the Pentecostal doctrine of subsequence. Also, a slight reinterpretation of *both* traditional Baptist doctrine *and* classical Pentecostal doctrine might bring them closer together and align them with the emphasis of BEM.

BEM admits that "Christians differ in their understanding as to where the sign of the gift of the Spirit is to be found."[3] Some traditions identify it with water baptism while others recognize the filling of the Holy Spirit as a *process* symbolized by several rites including baptism, anointing, and imposition of hands. This would seem to leave room for both the traditional Baptist view and a slightly modified form of the Pentecostal view.

Although most Baptist denominations and nearly all Pentecostal ones have not actively participated in ecumenical discussions (even with each other), some theologians have tried to bridge the gap between them. In doing so they may have provided some clues toward resolving differences all around. For example, Presbyterian-Pentecostal theologian J. Rodman Williams offers a constructive proposal leading toward a suggested synthesis (of doctrines on Spirit baptism) that will make

---

costal doctrine on this point see Donald W. Dayton, *Theological Roots of Pentecostalism* (Grand Rapids: Zondervan, 1987).

2. "Baptism," par. 14 in *Baptism, Eucharist and Ministry.*
3. Ibid.

possible serious mutual understanding and acceptance, if not total agreement, between traditional sacramental Christians, evangelicals (including Baptists), and Pentecostals.[4]

Williams suggests that "Baptism of (with, in) the Holy Spirit" be recognized by all parties as "not an addition to becoming a Christian (a view which sets up two categories of Christians), but [as] the climactic moment of entrance into Christian life." Thus, conversion (the initial event of salvation) and the gift of the Holy Spirit are two equally important *moments* of the one totality of Christian initiation and belong inseparably together. However, they may be separated in their actual occurrence. "Thus it is not proper to speak of Christians and Spirit-baptized Christians but only of persons in process of Christian initiation."[5]

Perhaps this understanding could be embraced by traditional sacramental Christians (Eastern Orthodox, Roman Catholic, Reformation Protestant), traditional evangelicals (including Baptists), and classical Pentecostals. The first two groups would have to recognize that the Pentecostal experience of baptism in the Holy Spirit (including glossolalia) may be a legitimate moment in the process of Christian initiation without giving up the truth that all Christians are forgiven, regenerated, and sealed by the Spirit as sons and daughters of God. For them, Agnes Ozman's experience of the "second blessing" would be interpreted as a genuine experience of inducement with power by the Holy Spirit consummating her initiation into Christ. They would in no way have to admit that such an experience is *necessary* for every Christian.

The group that would have the most trouble accepting this reinterpretation is the classical Pentecostals. However, many of them may be willing to admit that their "second blessing" experience is not a second, higher stage of Chris-

4. "Pentecostal Theology: A Neo-Pentecostal Viewpoint," in *Perspectives on the New Pentecostalism*, ed. Russell P. Spittler (Grand Rapids: Baker, 1967).
5. Ibid., p. 82.

tianity but a completion and consummation of the infilling of the Holy Spirit that Christians receive at conversion or in a process through sacramental rites.

A more intractable problem separating Pentecostals and other Christians is the doctrine of glossolalia as the necessary initial physical evidence of Spirit baptism. However, in practice if not in theory, many Pentecostals have already dropped the implication that it is necessary and are willing to admit that Christians (e.g., Billy Graham) who have never spoken in tongues may be truly Spirit-filled nonetheless.

POSSIBLE OUTCOMES

1. Pastor Williamson will not endorse the view that Agnes's experience ushered her into a higher stage of Christianity or was her first reception of the Spirit. He will continue to emphasize to her that she received the Holy Spirit when she first believed and was converted. However, he *may* admit that she had a fresh experience of the Holy Spirit at the Pentecostal church, which brought to completion something that *for her* was unfulfilled in her Christian initiation experience. Baptists traditionally talk about "rededication" of one's life to Christ. Pastor Williamson may interpret her experience (and others like it) as an ultimate rededication experience. He should not deny the validity of her experience, and he does not have to in order to remain faithful to either BEM or his Baptist beliefs.

2. Pastor Parham and his congregation should not attempt to proselytize Agnes away from her Baptist congregation. They should take satisfaction in the service they were able to give her in ushering her into a new experience of the Holy Spirit without in any way impugning her original conversion experience. They should at least emphasize to her that she *received* the Holy Spirit at conversion, a doctrine fully compatible with their own view of subsequent Baptism of the Holy Spirit.

3. The two pastors should meet to discuss their interpreta-

tions of Christian initiation and the role of the Holy Spirit in it, especially if Agnes' experience is repeated with other Baptists. Evangelicals like those at First Baptist Church and First Pentecostal Assembly have much in common. They should discuss whether they can accept something like J. Rodman Williams' view that Pentecostal Baptism of the Holy Spirit is a legitimate Christian experience that for many persons brings Christian initiation to its culmination.

4. It is highly unlikely that Baptists and Pentecostals will ever come to total agreement on these issues (especially that of speaking in tongues as initial evidence of Spirit baptism). However, they may and can come to agreement on how to help someone like Agnes Ozman who has had the Pentecostal experience but wants to remain a Baptist. Both will have to agree that Christian initiation does not necessarily follow a single pattern in every case.

CASE STUDIES ON EUCHARIST

5

Eucharistic Sharing at St. Pius

(Disciples/Roman Catholic)

JOHN T. FORD

Sister Derecha, the director of religious education at St. Pius Roman Catholic Church, was teaching the middle-school class in preparation for confirmation. One of the students asked if it would be alright to invite his Protestant neighbors to the confirmation ceremony. Sister Derecha replied that Protestants would be welcome to attend the ceremony, however they could not be invited to communion, "since only Catholics are allowed to receive communion."

Angela Antinomo promptly raised her hand and said, "My mother is a Protestant and she receives communion at Sunday mass." At first, Sister Derecha thought that Angela was mistaken, but when Angela insisted that her mother did receive communion, Sister Derecha decided to check with the pastor, Father Pregunta, who in turn contacted Mr. Antinomo.

In their subsequent conversation, Father Pregunta learned that Mr. Antinomo was a military officer; he and his wife had been married at a ceremony in which both her minister and his pastor had participated. Prior to their wedding, he and his wife had attended a pre-Cana conference and had agreed to rear their children as Catholics, although she had decided to remain a member of her own church, the Disciples of Christ.

The Antinomos had recently moved to the area in which St. Pius was located; previously they lived on a military base in the Midwest, where there were only two chaplains, one Catholic and the other a fundamentalist Protestant. The latter's theological mind-set and style of preaching soon persuaded Mrs. Antinomo to stop attending the Protestant services on base. Since there were no churches of the Disciples of Christ convenient to the base, she began to attend Sunday mass at the base on a regular basis.

Since communion is a regular part of the Sunday worship of the Disciples of Christ, Mrs. Antinomo asked the Catholic chaplain whether she might receive communion at mass. After learning that she believed that Christ is present at the eucharist, the chaplain told her to feel welcome to receive communion with her family. Such had been her practice for several years, and so she had continued to receive communion with her family at mass at St. Pius. However, about once a month, the family would attend a service at a Disciples church located about an hour from their home.

Mr. Antinomo told Father Pregunta that he felt that he was conscientiously fulfilling his promise to raise his children as Catholics while allowing his wife to follow her own conscience. He also felt that his family experienced the best of both churches: magnificent Gregorian chants at St. Pius and dynamic preaching at Riverside Christian Church.

He also felt that his family had been spared the disagreements about religion that frequently divided spouses in "mixed marriages." Indeed, he felt that their "ecumenical marriage" was training the children in a spirit of genuine Christian understanding and he hoped that what had proved so helpful for his own family could help other families in similar marriages.

Father Pregunta told Mr. Antinomo that he appreciated the Antinomo's special situation but he was unsure whether what they were doing was in accord with Roman Catholic canon law. When Mr. Antinomo asked why the Catholic chaplain had permitted his wife to start receiving communion at mass in the first place, Father Pregunta was at a loss for words.

Father Pregunta concluded the conversation by promising that he would check with Father Charla, the diocesan ecumenical officer, and Monsignor Ley, a canon lawyer in the chancery office, and then get back in touch.

DISCUSSION QUESTIONS

1. If you had been the Catholic military chaplain, would you have allowed Mrs. Antinomo to receive communion at mass? Why or why not?

2. If you were Father Charla, the diocesan ecumenical officer, what advice would you give to Father Pregunta?

3. If you were Monsignor Ley, what answer would you give to Father Pregunta's question about the provisions of canon law pertinent to this case?

4. If you were Father Pregunta, what pastoral approach would you take in advising Mr. Antinomo? What would you tell Sister Derecha? What would you tell Angela?

COMMENTARY

1. If you had been the Catholic military chaplain, would you have allowed Mrs. Antinomo to receive communion at mass? Why or why not?

The *Ecumenical Directory,* issued by the Vatican Secretariat for Promoting Christian Unity in 1967, permitted non-Catholic Christians to receive the sacraments of the eucharist, reconciliation, and anointing of the sick under very limited conditions: danger of death or urgent need, such as imprisonment or persecution.[1] A further instruction in 1972 somewhat broadened the understanding of what could be considered cases of urgent need to such situations as refugees in a foreign country. However, the interpretation of such "exceptions" in pastoral practice has varied from place to place, some pastors being more strict, others more flexible.

Apparently the Catholic military chaplain made the judgment that the combination of circumstances, including the lack of other religious opportunities on base, constituted a justifiable exception and so allowed Mrs. Antinomo to receive communion at mass.

2. If you were Father Charla, the diocesan ecumenical officer, what advice would you give to Father Pregunta?

Father Charla pointed out that the eucharist can be considered both as a sign of existing community and as a means toward further unity. In Mrs. Antinomo's case, her link with the Roman Catholic community is only partial insofar as she is not a Roman Catholic; nonetheless, her bond with the Catholic Church is very real, insofar as her family are practicing Catholics. Indeed, she really seems closer to the Roman Catholic Church than those nominal Catholics who attend mass only on special occasions like Christmas and Easter. In contrast, she regularly seeks to receive the eucharist as a means of spiritual nourishment.

Father Charla also emphasized that the Disciples of Christ-Roman Catholic Dialogue in the United States had "found sufficient theological justification for some eucharistic sharing"; indeed, that officially sponsored dialogue came to the conclusion that "urgent theological, ecumenical and especially pastoral reasons exist in our country to make some

1. The text of "The Directory Concerning Ecumenical Matters" (Part One) can be found in Thomas F. Stransky, C.S.P., and John B. Sheering, C.S.P., eds., *Doing the Truth in Charity: Statements of Pope Paul VI, Popes John Paul I, John Paul II, and the Secretariat for Promoting Christian Unity, 1964–1980* (New York: Paulist Press, 1982), pp. 41–57.

eucharistic sharing desirable."[2] Accordingly, the participants in that dialogue urged their respective "church bodies to explore as rapidly as possible the circumstances and procedures for responsible eucharistic sharing"[3]

While specific procedures for eucharistic sharing between Disciples and Roman Catholics have never been officially determined, Father Charla felt that in Mrs. Antinomo's case, there really is "sufficient theological justification for some eucharistic sharing." In addition, there seemed to be sufficient ecumenical and pastoral reasons to make an exception in her case. As for the canonical provisions, Father Charla suggested that Father Pregunta talk with an expert in canon law.

3. If you were Monsignor Ley, what answer would you give to Father Pregunta's question about the provisions of canon law pertinent to this case?

Monsignor Ley began his response by pointing out that to understand the canon law regarding the reception of the eucharist, one must keep in mind not only canonical principles and provisions but also their underlying theological premises.[4] In Roman Catholic theology, the eucharist is considered both an expression of full membership in the church and a source of spiritual nourishment for the individual.

In the case of Roman Catholics, this dual principle means that only those who are actual members and are properly disposed are to receive the eucharist. Proper preparation

2. "Summary Memorandum on Sharing the Eucharist" (April 29–May 1, 1968), in *Building Unity: Ecumenical Dialogues with Roman Catholic Participation in the United States,* ed. Joseph A. Burgess and Brother Jeffrey Gros, F.S.C. (Mahwah, N.J.: Paulist Press, 1989), p. 57.

3. "An Adventure in Understanding, 1967–1973," in *Building Unity,* p. 61.

4. Monsignor Ley's response is adapted from an article by James Provost, "Eucharistic Sharing from the Perspective of Roman Catholic Canon Law," in *Food for the Journey: Study on Eucharistic Sharing* (Albuquerque: National Association of Diocesan Ecumenical Officers, 1985), pp. 64–78.

includes the following: (1) a person is not conscious of grave sin (those who are guilty of serious sin are expected to refrain from receiving the eucharist until they have received the sacrament of reconciliation); (2) a person has an attitude of charity toward his or her neighbors; and (3) a person observes a fast of one hour before receiving the eucharist. As a minimum, Roman Catholics are required to receive communion at least once a year (usually during the Easter season) and to participate at mass on Sundays and holy days of obligation.

How does this same dual principle apply to non-Catholics? Are non-Roman Catholics ever permitted to receive communion in Roman Catholic churches? By way of exception, and for significant personal reasons, Vatican II allowed "spiritual and sacramental sharing" by those not in full communion with the Catholic Church. Provisions for this sharing were specified in the *Ecumenical Directory* in 1967, further described by the Vatican in 1972, and given definitive form in the new Code of Canon Law in 1983.

Canon 844 indicated that the eucharist is "open" only to those who are in full communion with the Roman Catholic Church. In effect, this canon rules out concelebration by Roman Catholic priests with ministers of churches not in communion with Rome. Nonetheless, this canon allows, under certain circumstances, the reception of the eucharist and the sacraments of reconciliation and anointing (1) by Catholics from other Christian ministers and (2) by other Christians from Catholics ministers:

- Roman Catholics may seek these sacraments from a non–Roman Catholic minister under two conditions: first, a Roman Catholic minister must be inaccessible; second, the minister from whom a Roman Catholic seeks the sacrament must be validly ordained (canon 844, #2; determination of the validity of orders of other churches is reserved to Rome, which has recognized the validity of orders in the Orthodox churches).

- In the case of members of the Orthodox and Oriental churches, Roman Catholic ministers may licitly administer the sacraments of penance, eucharist, and anointing of the sick if members of these churches are properly disposed and ask for these sacraments on their own initiative (canon 844, #3). These sacraments may also be administered to members of other churches, which in the judgment of the Vatican are in the same situation as the eastern churches as far as these sacraments are concerned. (Two factors argue against a broader interpretation of this provision: (a) the canon specifies the validity of the sacraments in the minister's church, not simply the validity of the sacraments in virtue of the minister's own orders; (b) Rome regularly requires the ordination of ministers from Reformation churches who wish to become Roman Catholic priests.)

- In the case of members of other churches, Roman Catholic ministers may administer these sacraments to other Christians not in full communion with Rome under the following conditions: (a) the person is a baptized Christian; (b) the person feels a serious need for the sacraments (judgment about such "serious need" is the prerogative of the diocesan bishop or the conference of bishops); (c) access to a minister of one's own communion is not possible; (d) the person requests the sacraments on his or her own initiative; (e) the person has a Catholic belief in the sacraments; (f) the person has an appropriate disposition (similar to that expected of a Catholic approaching the sacraments) (canon 844, #4).

- Exceptions can be made on a case by case basis or codified into general norms by a diocesan bishop or an episcopal conference (canon 844, #5). If there are no general norms, and if consultation with the diocesan bishop is impossible in a particular situation, it seems appropriate to consider the purpose of the law, specifically the fact that the revised code allows exceptions for the spiritual welfare of individuals who seek to receive the sacraments.

After this detailed presentation, Monsignor Ley summarized the applicable provisions of canon law (844, #4). Obviously, Mrs. Antinomo is a baptized Christian who feels a serious need for receiving communion regularly; in addition, attending both St. Pius and Riverside Church every Sunday is practically impossible; the desire to receive communion is her own; and she knows, through her family, both the Catholic teaching on the eucharist and the dispositions necessary for receiving it. The pastoral question then is whether her spiritual need is serious enough to warrant an exception.

Father Pregunta might make this decision on his own, or he might feel obliged to consult his bishop.

4. If you were Father Pregunta, what pastoral approach would you take in advising Mrs. Antinomo? What would you tell Sister Derecha? What would you tell Angela?

Father Pregunta felt very uncomfortable with the dilemma in which he found himself. On the one hand, he instinctively agreed with Sister Derecha that the eucharist is a sign of the community of faith among members of the Roman Catholic Church and, accordingly, only Catholics should be admitted to communion. On the other hand, he personally treasured the eucharist as a source of spiritual nourishment; thus, he sympathized with Mrs. Antinomo's desire to receive the eucharist every Sunday.

Father Pregunta also felt an obligation to the parishioners of St. Pius: what would they think about his giving communion to someone whom he knew was a Protestant? Would they be scandalized? Father Pregunta tried to decide whether the need for the good order of the Catholic community would outweigh the spiritual needs not only of Mrs. Antinomo but also of the other members of her family, who might not wish to receive the eucharist if she were not permitted to receive.

Finally, what made Father Pregunta most uncomfortable was the feeling that whatever he decided to do, some would misunderstand his decision; it was difficult enough to sort out the issues for himself, but how would he ever be able to explain his decision to his parishioners? And if he decided not to allow Mr. Antinomo to receive communion, how would he explain his decision to his colleagues in the ministerial association? But worst of all, how would he ever be able to explain a negative decision to the youngsters in the confirmation class, much less to Angela?

Father Pregunta recognized that he was in a problematic situation, so he tried to imagine the possible outcomes of various decisions that he might make.

POSSIBLE OUTCOMES

1. Father Pregunta might decide that it would be best to let matters continue as they have been. Presumably the military chaplain decided that Mrs. Antinomo should be considered an exception; moreover, it would seriously disrupt the family's religious life by asking Mrs. Antinomo to stop receiving communion. But then he would have to ask Sister Derecha to consider Mrs. Antinomo an "exception" without extending the same privilege to others.

2. Father Pregunta would have been happiest had the question not arisen but now that it has been publicly raised, he feels he must consult the bishop. If the bishop decides that Mrs. Antinomo can be considered an exception under the provisions of canon 844, #4, then Father Pregunta could tell Mrs. Antinomo that she has received permission from the bishop to receive communion with her family. Such a response would obviously satisfy Sister Derecha as well.

3. Father Pregunta also realized that if he consulted the bishop, the bishop might decide that Mrs. Antinomo must be told that she must either become a Roman Catholic or refrain from receiving the eucharist in the future. On a fair day, Father Pregunta could imagine himself persuading Mrs. Antinomo that it would be ideal if she would decide to be confirmed as a Roman Catholic along with her daughter, Angela.

4. On the other hand, it might be a cloudy day; Father Pregunta could imagine himself inviting Mrs. Antinomo to take instructions in Catholicism so that she could be confirmed along with her daughter. A few days after that interview, Sister Derecha might well call to ask whether Father Pregunta knew that Angela Antinomo has stopped attending confirmation class.

If you were Father Pregunta, what would you do?

6

Mission of the Atonement

(Lutheran/Roman Catholic)

DALE JAMTGAARD

In the later months of 1985, the congregation of Atonement Lutheran Church came to realize that its survival was in jeopardy. The income was not adequate to meet expenses. Of the options presented, the congregation decided to look for another Christian congregation that wanted to rent the church facilities part-time.

The Lutheran pastor was on friendly terms with one of the auxiliary bishops of the Roman Catholic Archdiocese of Portland and from them an idea emerged. The Bishop visited a neighboring parish, St. Anthony's Catholic Church, and in meetings with the laity, he invited them to form a mission community. They established it at the Atonement Lutheran facilities.

What evolved was more than anyone anticipated. The Lutherans and Catholics met together and elected to form one community of two traditions, each maintaining its separate identity.

The idea was met warmly by about 60 percent of the Lutheran congregation. Some were uncertain as to what was happening but saw no alternative. Some wanted no part of it. Others were willing to try it, and the rest were enthusiastic.

The bishop of the North Pacific District of the American Lutheran Church was hesitant but told them to proceed with caution. He visited the church and became supportive of the new venture, but shortly after that he died of a heart attack. The formation of the Evangelical Lutheran Church in America resulted in the election of a new bishop who has given encouragement to the then year-and-a-half old mission.

The archbishop of the archdiocese of Portland was supportive during the initial phase. He then left and a new archbishop came onto the scene with the community already established and operating. The new archbishop remained cautious, taking time to acquaint himself with the nature of the intent. His support has grown with time.

The Catholic laity who chose to come from St. Anthony's came with enthusiasm. Many of them had held leadership positions in that parish. There were varied degrees of support and non-support from the other neighboring parishes, both Lutheran and Roman Catholic.

Questions that needed answers

There were five major issues that demanded attention as the two churches sought to share as much as we could yet remain true to our respective church bodies.

1. To what extent could we share our public worship life, i.e., the liturgy of the Word, prayer, eucharist, festival services, marriages, and baptisms?

2. How could we emphasize the laity's role in public ministry yet maintain a balance of lay and clergy leadership that would be effective and acceptable to each church body?

3. What patterns of administrative and financial support would be acceptable and effective for both communities given the differences in our traditions?

4. Which educational programs did we want to do cooperatively and which did we deem necessary to do independently?

5. Since we wanted to maintain the interest and support of the Archdiocese of Portland and the Lutheran North Pacific District and subsequently the Oregon Synod, what role would they exercise in the decision making?

Worship, the first concern

When our community began, the major concern was how we could all worship together. It seemed important to both the Lutherans and the Roman Catholics that we find some way in which we could gather together on Sunday morning to celebrate as one community of Christians. This desire was balanced by our concern that we not just form some new style of church but that we remain faithful to our respective traditions and thus serve as an ongoing expression of ecumenism between the two church bodies.

The community had some difficulty in deciding on the format for our joint services. It was the unanimous desire of the members of the community that we celebrate the eucharist together. However, this proved to be impossible, given the regulations on pulpit and altar fellowship for both the Roman Catholic and Lutheran Churches. We had originally hoped that we would be allowed to hold, in the same room and preferably at the same altar, a joint liturgy of the word with separate consecrations and communions. We soon found out that this was not acceptable to either church authority.

Our final solution for a total joint service, although it is considered somewhat less than ideal by many members of the community, was to hold a common liturgy of the Word on the final Sunday of each month. Consistent with a commitment to lay leadership, it was decided that lay people would lead this service and also preach.

There still remained the problem of the other Sundays. Ideally, many people wanted to hold a joint service of the Word on those Sundays, and then separate for eucharistic services. Separating into two rooms for the eucharist raised the issue of whether the eucharist was different in importance than the liturgy of the Word. Both traditions hold that Christ is equally present in Word and sacrament. In the past the Roman Catholic Church has tended to give the eucharist more prominence in worship, and the Lutheran Church has tended to favor the liturgy of the Word. Therefore the unity of the process now seems important for both. It was then reasoned that, when both Word and sacrament are a part of a worship service, the policy of separation for the eucharist should apply to the liturgy of the Word also. This is an issue that we believe would be worthy of further consideration.

After some experimentation, we decided to hold a very short "entrance" service of song and prayer each Sunday (except for the last Sunday of the month) and then separate for the entire Lutheran liturgy and Catholic mass. The two groups alternate between using the sanctuary and the fellowship hall. Before the separation, which is always acknowledged as painful, the two groups sing a blessing to each other.

Lay people lead the joint service and the short opening services and the two pastors jointly conduct the liturgy of the Word for baptisms, weddings, and other special occasions. Each Monday the clergy and laity meet jointly for text study and the planning of the liturgies.

Christian Education

From the founding of the mission, Christian education has been considered a function to be conducted jointly to the extent possible. Children's Sunday school and adult classes are offered for one hour, three to four Sundays per month. On the last Sunday of each month a community potluck brunch replaces both adult and children's education.

Curriculum for the weekly children's Sunday school — preschool through junior high — emphasizes Bible study on common beliefs and values and avoids emphasis on doctrinal differences. Whenever possible, two teachers work as a team with each group. Currently, we offer a first communion and first reconciliation program for both Lutheran and Roman

Catholic children and a confirmation program for Lutheran children.

Joint adult education offerings have been very popular. Topics have been varied, including an extensive overview of the Lutheran/Catholic dialogues and more detailed discussion of specific topics such as justification by faith, an overview of church history, a series on prayer, a discussion series on differing liturgical and non-liturgical traditions, and Bible studies.

Evening classes have been held on holistic health, interpersonal relationships, and family issues. In addition, Pastor Dale Jamtgaard has been developing material and methods for a new small group spiritual and personal growth program called "Faithwalk." This involves members of the community and also serves as an outreach program. "Couples of Two Religious Traditions" is a unique study and fellowship group that explores the challenges faced by such ecumenical couples in their marriages and in educating their children.

We have also sponsored an ecumenical workshop in which both the Catholic archbishop and the Lutheran bishop have made presentations and given their support.

Administration

The Lutheran and Roman Catholic communities each have councils consisting of the clergy and six elected lay representatives. These councils meet separately, when needed, but most administrative decisions are made at the meetings of the monthly community council, which combines these two groups. The Lutheran community is a separate religious nonprofit corporation and because of the history of the mission, it owns the church building. The Catholic community is technically viewed as a mission of neighboring St. Anthony's Parish, but practically operates in most respects like a separate parish.

Active lay involvement has been a key aspect of the mission. Both pastors are part-time. They work with the standing committees for ministry in the areas of liturgy and worship, outreach and hospitality, administration and finance, Christian education, ecumenical concerns, social action, and fun.

We held a balance of lay and clergy leadership for worship as a goal from the beginning. This was further established during the year in which we were without permanent clergy, for the visiting clergy provided minimal coverage. The lay men and women then assumed the primary responsibility for the joint service, including presiding and preaching. Today the laity also assist with the liturgy and eucharist in the separate services. This seems to be well accepted. Both communities are concerned with providing adequate preparation for these roles and are seeking to do this jointly.

The two pastors who began this cooperative venture resigned from both the mission and the clerical status within the first year. In the selection of clergy, each community followed its own process with little involvement from the other community. However, we would change this in the future to provide for more shared input.

Father Matthias Tumulty serves half-time at the mission and half-time as the director of the Franciscan Enterprise, which rehabilitates and rents low-income housing. Pastor Dale Jamtgaard also serves the mission half-time and has a half-time private counseling practice as a clinical social worker.

The different approaches to compensating clergy and the related need for financial support for the mission as a whole provided an education for both communities. Pastor Dale's compensation package includes a salary, a housing and car allowance, and pension contributions. Although his compensation is below the church guidelines, it is substantially higher than Catholic parishes would ordinarily pay a priest. Father Matt is paid a monthly stipend, which only covers a portion of his living expenses.

Despite the substantial differences in clergy compensation, the Catholic community readily agreed to support the community budget. Both communities have learned about the differences in attitudes and methods of supporting the church. Catholics have experienced and learned to appreciate the more active Lutheran approach to stewardship. Average contributions by Catholics have substantially increased, although they are still below the level of average Lutheran contributions. A large percentage of members of both communities give a high level of support in contributions of time and talents.

Unfortunately, the Lutheran community had lost membership because of the difficulties prior to the formation of the mission and experienced some mixed feelings at its inception. Even with the joint community, the income was not adequate to meet the pared down expenses. Some neighboring Lutheran congregations have responded with contributions. We have now received an equal commitment from each church body of a two-year subsidy, after which we plan to be self-supporting.

The communities have also learned of their differing approaches to membership. Catholics emphasize membership in the diocese, while membership in a Catholic parish has little or no formality and consists primarily of being listed on the parish register. Lutherans, on the other hand, identify much more strongly with their membership in and commitment to a particular congregation. For Lutherans the joining of a parish is achieved in a more formal way than for Catholics.

We hold orientation classes and a reception for new members both to respect the Lutheran tradition and to give prospective members a greater appreciation of the unique nature of the mission. However, both are optional, out of regard for the less formal Catholic tradition. The welcoming of new members is done at a gathering of both communities to recognize the participation in a larger mission.

A concern of the community is that although we are doing well in participation, service, and stewardship, we need to grow in order to be fully self-supporting. Finding others who are enthusiastic about our joint venture is difficult. More Catholics have shown an interest than Lutherans and our best resource, not surprisingly, is couples of mixed religious traditions. Their need is an area we feel we are uniquely positioned to serve.

Reflections

We feel privileged to experience ecumenism on a weekly basis. Both communities have come to appreciate what the other tradition has to contribute to the richness of the worship, fellowship, and service of our community. We share an even greater appreciation, however, in the sense of oneness of the Church as we experience our unity in Christ.

When we realize the importance of our unity in Christ, we see our differences in an appropriate perspective. While it is important to have ways to deal with the differences, we believe we also need settings where our unity in Christ is acknowledged and celebrated. This we believe is our contribution to the movement of ecumenism.

Given the years of conflict and distrust between the Roman Catholic and Lutheran Churches, we like to say to all who come, "Welcome to a miracle."

DISCUSSION QUESTIONS

1. As a Lutheran, would you be willing to be part of a mission community with Roman Catholics?

2. As a Roman Catholic, would you be willing to be part of a mission community with Lutherans?

3. How would belonging to such a mission community affect your idea of "church membership"?

4. What common understanding of the eucharist do Lutherans and Roman Catholics share?

5. What prevents Lutherans and Roman Catholics from sharing the eucharist?

7

Longing for the Table of the Lord

(Presbyterian/Episcopal)

AURELIA T. FULE

Tom Walker was not certain what he was going to do with the rest of his life, but he wanted to be useful to others. As soon as he graduated from Swarthmore College he volunteered for Habitat for Humanity, where he could be productive and have time to think about the future. He liked the company of the other young and some not-so-young volunteers, and enjoyed many of the families for whom they were building homes. Tom grew in his experience as a volunteer: he developed physically, he became more at ease with strangers, he sensed a feeling of belonging, or solidarity, with his fellow volunteers, and his faith deepened as he worked with some very dedicated people.

Before Tom completed his term as a volunteer he knew what he was called to do. He applied to three seminaries. Two accepted him, and he chose Yale Divinity School. Although Yale is a nondenominational seminary and Tom was Presbyterian, he could become a candidate for ministry under the guidance of his regional governing board, or presbytery.

During his time in seminary, Tom found himself drawn to the weekly seminary communion service and began to attend it frequently. By the middle of his second year, he never missed

71

weekly communion, and whenever he was away from school he felt that worship without communion was lacking something. That summer, far from home and far from Yale, he attended the Episcopal church in town for its communion service every week.

Two months after graduation, Tom received a call from a Presbyterian church in rural Ohio. He liked the place and the people and accepted the call. He was ordained and installed to the ministry in Ohio and started eagerly.

Tom's enthusiasm faltered when he found that his new church celebrated communion only once a month. The congregation had previously observed communion four times a year and, after much coaxing by their former pastor, had moved to monthly communion. But for Tom once a month was not enough; he longed for the weekly communion services that had become such an integral part of his worship. The Lord's Supper, he felt, placed him firmly in the Church between Christ's incarnation and return, as the words of 1 Corinthians 11 express: "as often as you eat this bread and drink this cup you proclaim till he come."

Tom decided to appeal to the church governing board, or session, about holding communion more frequently. Armed with his knowledge of John Calvin's writings from seminary, he read to the session passages from *Theological Treatises*, where Calvin argues that "it would be well to require that the Communion of the Holy Supper of Jesus Christ be held every Sunday at least as a rule."[1] Tom then discussed 1 Corinthians 11 and similar scriptural passages, but the session would not move. Some members clearly felt that monthly communion was already too frequent. Greater frequency, they argued, would make participation less special.

Uncertain about what he should do next, Tom sought counsel from some of his older colleagues and from the chair of the Ministerial and Church Relations Committee, but no

---

1. John Calvin, "Articles concerning the Organization of the Church and of Worship at Geneva (1537)" in *Calvin: Theological Treatises*, ed. John K. S. Reid (Philadelphia: Westminster Press, 1977), p. 48.

one shared his need for communion or understood his spiritual hunger sufficiently. Some days after a disappointing talk with an older colleague, he traveled to a nearby town and spoke with the priest at the Episcopalian church, who welcomed him to the table.

Tom began to visit the church for weekly communion and soon felt more settled. He would not give up on the session. He would continue to make references to communion but realized it was a long, long road. After all, even Calvin could not persuade the people of Geneva.

Soon it became known that Tom attended the Episcopalian church midweek to receive communion. Members of the session were disturbed; some even said they felt betrayed. They asked Tom to stop the practice, but Tom would promise no such thing. Finally, Tom and the session agreed to turn to the presbytery for counsel.

DISCUSSION QUESTIONS

1. Why did Tom feel that he needed communion?

2. Could Tom have found a better way of persuading the session to agree to try holding the Lord's Supper "every Sunday at least as a rule"?

3. Was Tom seeking something that is alien to his own tradition? Or peripheral to the tradition of the Church catholic?

4. Why do people oppose weekly communion?

5. Why were people unwilling to try weekly communion for a time? (People do not miss good music if they have never heard it, but once they have learned to like it, they will miss it. Is the same true for communion?)

6. Why did some people feel "betrayed" when they learned about Tom's communion at the Episcopal church?

7. What might happen in your congregation in a similar case?

8. What may be considered an offense concerning the eucharist in your community?

COMMENTARY

Tom was sure of the depth of his longing for communion, but he wanted a firm understanding of why it was important to him before he appeared before the presbytery. At the suggestion of a denominational staff member for ecumenical relations, he contacted Alethea Truest at the World Council of Churches' Office of Faith and Order for advice on where he could find a discussion of the churches' positions on communion.

Alethea directed Tom to the WCC's *Baptism, Eucharist and Ministry* statement and the Consultation on Church Union, both of which Tom was already familiar with. Giving him a copy of a report from the Anglican-Reformed International Consultation as well, Alethea suggested that in these three documents Tom might find answers to his questions about the Lord's Supper.

Tom began reading and learned the following from each document:

Baptism, Eucharist and Ministry

Beginning with the most inclusive statement, BEM asked the churches "the extent to which your church can recognize in this text the faith of the Church through the ages." According to BEM, the eucharist, which always includes *both* Word and sacrament, is understood as

- thanksgiving to the Father
- *anamnesis* or memorial of Christ
- invocation of the Spirit
- communion of the faithful
- meal of the Kingdom[2]

2. See "Eucharist" in *Baptism, Eucharist and Ministry*.

74

In regard to the question of frequency, BEM stated that "as the eucharist celebrates the resurrection of Christ, it is appropriate that it should take place at least every Sunday ("Eucharist," par. 31).

Consultation on Church Union

In its *Consensus,* approved in 1984, the Consultation on Church Union understood the Lord's Supper "as including the preaching of the Word" (15). Although using different terminology, the *COCU Consensus* describes the celebration of the Lord's Supper in terms parallel to BEM:

- Christ's high priestly act of sacrifice gathers up our self-offerings of praise, thanksgiving, and service and unites them with his own (16). The bread and cup are taken, they are blessed as thanks is given over them for God's creation and redemption of the world in Christ (18).
- The sacrament of the Lord's Supper proclaims and recalls the life, death, and resurrection of Christ (15).
- The act of giving thanks includes prayer invoking the Holy Spirit (18).
- The Lord's Supper, wherever it is celebrated, is the communion of the universal Church of God (17).
- The sacrament of the Lord's Supper proclaims and recalls the life, death, and resurrection of Christ while looking forward to Christ's return (15).[3]

In 1989, the Consultation issued *Churches in Covenant Communion,* which speaks of the sacrament of the Lord's Supper with reference to BEM, lists the same five elements, and defines them in terms of near quotation from BEM.[4] Such

---

3. Gerald F. Moede, ed., *The COCU Consensus: In Quest of a Church of Christ Uniting* (Princeton, N.J.: Consultation on Church Union, 1985); references in parentheses are to the numbered paragraphs of Chapter 6, "Worship."

4. *Churches in Covenant Communion* (Princeton, N.J.: Consultation on Church Union, 1988).

citation is not merely stylistic, Tom noted, but is an indication that reception has taken place.

The Anglican-Reformed International Commission

This international dialogue, whose members were appointed by the Anglican Consultative Council and the World Alliance of Reformed Churches, stated the following in its report, *God's Reign and Our Unity:*[5]

- The eucharist is a memorial *(anamnesis)* of the unique sacrifice of Christ (65). The preached word is an *(anamnesis)* of Christ just as is the eucharistic meals (67).
- Invocation *(epiklesis)* is a proper part of the eucharistic action (68).
- The eucharist is constitutive of the Church because in it Christ unites the disciples with himself (64).
- The eucharist unites us with Christ, with one another, and with the whole company of Christ's people in every age and place (70).
- The presence of the Spirit is the foretaste, pledge, and first-fruits of God's coming kingdom (69).

The affirmations agree with BEM, but no mention is made of thanksgiving. However, the term eucharist (thanksgiving) may have been considered sufficient without elaboration.

On frequency of communion, the Commission stated that the celebration of the sacrament is "the proper form of worship for . . . the Lord's day" and "should be accepted as the norm in both traditions" (71).

Encouraged by the support he found in these three documents, Tom turned next to the book that is most normative in Presbyterian worship.

5. *God's Reign and Our Unity,* The Report of the Anglican-Reformed International Commission 1981–1984, Woking, England, January 1984 (London: SPCK, 1984).

The Presbyterian Church (U.S.A.)

In the Presbyterian Church (U.S.A.), the current Directory for Worship, adopted by the 201st General Assembly in 1989, devotes almost four pages to the Lord's Supper. Tom found that the summaries of five paragraphs clearly correspond to the affirmations in BEM. The Lord's Supper is

- Thanksgiving
- Remembering
- Invocation
- Community of the Faithful
- Foretaste of the Kingdom Meal

(W2.4000–4012)

Concerning frequency, the Directory for Worship states that "It is appropriate to celebrate the Lord's Supper as often as each Lord's Day" (W2.4009).

This parallelism between the Presbyterian Directory for Worship and BEM reminded Tom of the response to BEM adopted by the Presbyterian Church (U.S.A.) at its 198th General Assembly in 1986. This response affirmed the five elements highlighted and expressed support for "the increasing emphasis upon more frequent communion" within the Presbyterian Church (U.S.A.).[6]

In fact, Tom found in further research that the eucharistic theology expressed in both the Presbyterian response to BEM and the Directory for Worship was evident in the predecessors of the current Directory for Worship that were adopted by the United Presbyterian Church in the U.S.A. in 1967 and the Presbyterian Church in the United States in 1963. (These

---

6. Max Thurian, ed., *Churches Respond to BEM: Official Responses to the "Baptism, Eucharist and Ministry" Text*, Volume III. Faith and Order Paper 135 (Geneva: World Council of Churches, 1987), pp. 189–205. In general, this response is one of receptivity to the BEM statement on baptism and eucharist and, to a lesser extent, to its statement on ministry.

churches, which had split during the Civil War, were reunited in 1983 to form the Presbyterian Church [U.S.A.].)

In reading the two older documents Tom saw that the chapters on the Lord's Supper in both Directories recognize the first four elements highlighted in BEM. The fifth element, "meal of the Kingdom," has no corresponding phrase, but the United Presbyterian Church Directory speaks of the Lord's Supper as one in which God offers "the continued spiritual nourishment upon which . . . eternal life depends" (21.01).

In regard to frequency of celebration, the UPC Directory states that "It is fitting . . . as frequently as on each Lord's Day" (21.01), and the Presbyterian Church, U.S., Directory recommends that communion "be celebrated frequently . . . at least quarterly" (211–12).

Tom's brief review of the eucharistic theology of BEM and the current Directory for Worship revealed that recent ecumenical discussions have provided not so much content as clarity of formulation. Tom could only wonder whether earlier ecumenical discussions might have influenced the predecessors of the current Directory. In any event, he realized, what BEM has contributed is a greater awareness of what could be owned by the Church catholic.

Satisfied with what he had found in the Presbyterian Church's documents, Tom reviewed John Calvin's position on communion.

John Calvin (1509–1564)

Reading Calvin and other Reformers on the Lord's Supper took Tom not only to another age (the sixteenth century) but to another discussion. The Reformers rejected the Roman Catholic doctrine of transubstantiation — the belief that ordinary bread and wine are transformed in their substance so that Christ is actually present in them.

Instead, Calvin and other Reformers sought to explain how Christ is spiritually present in the eucharist. Reacting to what seemed to him to be Roman Catholic malpractice in the

celebration of the eucharist, Calvin affirmed the Lord's Supper
(1) to be part of the worship service; (2) to include the proclamation of the Word; (3) to include the participation of the
congregation (i.e., not private communion); (4) to affirm the
true presence of Christ in the sacrament of the Lord's Supper.[7]

These elements are present not only in Calvin but also in
BEM because they belong to the Church catholic. But, Tom
wondered, have the highlighted elements of BEM been present
in the Reformed tradition from the beginning? In his *Instruction in Faith* and *Institutes of the Christian Religion*, Calvin
made the following remarks concerning the Lord's Supper:[8]

Thanksgiving

"God's liberality . . . is so great toward us in the sacrament
that we need . . . to extol it with fitting praises and to
celebrate it with thanksgiving" (*Instruction*, 68–69).

Remembering

"The sacrament sends us to the cross of Christ" (*Institutes*,
4.17.4).

Invocation

"The power of the Holy Spirit towers above all our senses"
(*Institutes*, 4.17.10).

7. See John Calvin, "Short Treatise on the Lord's Supper" in *Calvin:
Theological Treatises,* ed. John K. S. Reid (Philadelphia: Westminster
Press, 1977), pp. 142–166.

8. Calvin, *Instruction in Faith,* ed. Paul T. Fuhrmann (Louisville,
Ky.: Westminster/John Knox, 1992), pp. 68–69; and *Institutes of the
Christian Religion,* ed. John T. McNeill, trans. Ford Lewis Battles
(Philadelphia: Westminster Press, 1960). References in parentheses are
to book, chapter, paragraph.

Communion of the Faithful

"[The sacrament] conjoins together the members of one same body . . . in as much as [Christ] makes himself common to all, he makes us also one in himself" (*Instruction*, 68–69).

Meal of the Kingdom

This element is not found in Calvin, but a phrase opening to the future is used often: "by these foods [Christ's body and blood] believers are nourished unto eternal life" (*Institutes*, 4.17.8).

Concerning frequency of communion, Calvin wrote that "It would be well to require that the Communion of the Holy Supper of Jesus Christ be held every Sunday at least as a rule."[9]

Tom was ready to sum up what he had learned. He would present the following conclusions to the presbytery.

Conclusions

For the Presbyterian Church (U.S.A.), the affirmations concerning the eucharist highlighted in BEM were matters recognized as the faith of the Church throughout the ages, including the Reformed tradition. Therefore, although some features of BEM called Presbyterians to rethink certain matters, the reception of BEM is not something new or hitherto not discovered. But that is not all.

First, BEM influenced both the phrasing as well as the order and clarity of the two most recent COCU documents, *COCU Consensus* and *Churches in Covenant Community*, as well as the current Directory for Worship of the Presbyterian Church (U.S.A.).

9. Calvin, "Articles Concerning the Organization of the Church" in *Calvin: Theological Treatises,* ed. John K. S. Reid (Philadelphia: Westminster Press, 1954), p. 48.

Secondly, seeing how strongly the tradition values the significance and frequency of the Lord's Supper, the question might be asked, Why is this not evident in most Protestant congregations? Reception of this tradition has taken place in many of the member churches of Faith and Order and the World Council of Churches on the highest authority levels. Where it has yet to take place is the local congregation.

POSSIBLE OUTCOMES

After hearing Tom's argument in support of weekly communion, the presbytery's ministry committee concluded that not only had Tom not broken any church laws or betrayed his congregation, but he was fulfilling a responsibility he had for his own spiritual nurture as well as that of the congregation.

The ministry committee made suggestions to both Tom and the session for resolving the issue. To the session, the ministry committee advised that it might (1) have two communion services each month for the next year and then reconsider the matter; (2) send the youth group to summer camp, where communion is celebrated twice a week, and then invite the youth members to share their experience with the congregation.

To Tom, the ministry committee recommended that he try one of the following options: (1) offer four lectures and discussions on the theology of the Lord's Supper as part of the adult education program; (2) invite other Presbyterian pastors, whose congregation had weekly communion, to speak at his parish.

Finally, the committee suggested that if Tom found these efforts unrewarded, he might want to consider looking for another pastorate.

8

A Communion Service at Petitville

(Methodist/Roman Catholic)

JOHN T. FORD

Reverend Rex Sarcinator was the first full-time pastor in the century-long history of Petitville United Methodist Church. For most of its existence, Petitville had been a pleasant country village with a few stores and a few hundred citizens, but in recent years, as the suburbs moved out from the city, new families began moving in. Petitville United Methodist, the only church in town, had previously been served as part of a three-point charge (three small congregations served by the same pastor).

Recognizing the opportunities for church growth, Bishop Leo Leiter decided to appoint a full-time pastor to reach out to new members. Although recently ordained, Rex seemed an ideal choice; his family roots were rural, yet because he had spent twenty years in the military before beginning his studies for the Methodist ministry, he was familiar with many parts of the United States.

More than fulfilling Bishop Leiter's hopes, Rex was able to use the experiences of his rural childhood as a point of contact with the "old-time" members of the church, while his wide-ranging travels as a military officer enabled him to converse readily with "new arrivals." This is not to say, however, that there was no tension between the two groups.

The old-timers, while grateful that the church's increasing membership had finally enabled them to have a full-time pastor, were somewhat uneasy about the "liberal" ideas of some of the new members. The latter, while glad to live in a community of "good neighbors," were occasionally dismayed by their "conservative" outlook. Rex managed to serve as a bridge between the two groups; indeed, he saw the inevitable tensions as offering creative possibilities for reaching out to everyone in the village.

Rex made it part of his ministry to welcome every new family that moved into the village. It was on one such visit that he met Jude and Judy Weihen. When he invited them to attend the next Sunday's service, he saw them exchange glances, then hesitate about accepting; however, they did attend the service the following Sunday and several subsequent services as well. After they had attended regularly for several months, Rex asked Jude and Judy whether they would be interested in working on any of the church's committees.

Judy carefully replied, "We'd like to, but we had better talk about it."

When Rex met privately with the couple, they began by saying how much they enjoyed the worship at the church, the friendliness of its members, and particularly the warm welcome that they had received from Rex.

"But there may be a problem with our joining," said Jude. "I am a former Roman Catholic priest and Judy was the director of religious education in my parish."

Rex thanked them for their honesty and then said, "Petitville Church could certainly use your training and experience. Quite frankly, I'd like to have your assistance in whatever ways you feel comfortable helping."

It was not long before Judy was teaching Sunday school and Jude was working with the youth group. Rex also called upon them to participate in the service as readers and commentators. Rex found Jude to be a person with whom he could talk about "church problems," while Judy and Rex's wife, Ruth, soon became great friends. For Jude and Judy, it was a gratifying opportunity to resume ministries that they had once cherished.

On the morning of World Communion Sunday, Ruth telephoned Jude to tell him that Rex had come down with the flu and was too sick to get out of bed. "Would you be willing to lead the service?"

Jude agreed but wondered, "Fine, but what about the communion service?"

Rex replied over the extension, "Wouldn't it be incongruous to celebrate World Communion Sunday without communion? In fact, the whole service is already printed in the program. Would you be willing to conduct the communion service? After all, you've celebrated communion more often than I have."

Jude agreed to celebrate the communion service as planned. However, at the beginning of the eucharistic part of the service, Jude briefly mentioned the fact that he had been ordained as a Roman Catholic but had left the priesthood, that this was the first time since then that he had presided at a communion service, and that he was pleased to do so at Rex's invitation.

When Jude pronounced the final benediction, he almost cried. He told the congregation that it was not only a great personal privilege but most of all a symbol of the friendship that he and Judy had experienced in the church. It was a deeply moving experience for the church members, most of whom embraced Jude and Judy as they left the service.

Not everyone was happy, however. Ira and Irene Petit, whose ancestors had founded both the village and the church, did not receive communion nor did they even pause to shake hands with Jude and Judy after the service. A few days later, Mr. and Mrs. Petit met with Bishop Leiter and asked, "How could you possibly permit a Roman Catholic priest to celebrate mass in *our* Methodist church?"

DISCUSSION QUESTIONS

1. What is the difference between "mass" and "communion service"?

2. What importance does the celebration of the eucharist have in your church? How frequently is the eucharist celebrated?

3. Who is authorized to celebrate the eucharist in your church?

4. Is a person who is ordained in another denomination ever permitted to celebrate the eucharist for members of your denomination?

5. If you were Bishop Leiter, what would you do in this situation?

Investigation

Bishop Leiter, who was well aware that the Petit family had been one of the financial mainstays of the Petitville Church, assured Ira and Irene that he would investigate the matter thoroughly.

Barely recovered from his bout with flu, Rex was soon in the bishop's office. After describing the circumstances that led him to ask Jude to preside at the communion service, Rex concluded, "The programs were already printed."

Bishop Leiter was not satisfied. "Why couldn't you have saved them until later and simply used the regular worship books?"

Rex replied, "We don't have enough worship books. We have deferred purchasing more books until we can buy all new copies — instead the service is printed in a weekly program. But more importantly, it was World Communion Sunday."

Bishop Leiter insisted, "In the past Petitville Church never had communion more than two or three times a year."

"Sad, but true," Rex responded. "But that doesn't mean that communion shouldn't be more frequent. After all, regular communion is very much a part of the Methodist tradition."

When Bishop Leiter expressed some surprise at this statement, Rex warmed to the topic. "Like other Protestants, we have allowed the pulpit to obscure the altar. Now, without minimizing at all the preaching of God's word, we more clearly recognize the equivalent place of the sacrament."

"Where did you get such an idea?" asked the bishop.

Rex smiled. "From the official response of the United Methodist Church to the World Council of Churches' document on *Baptism, Eucharist and Ministry*."[1]

The bishop quickly headed the conversation in another direction. "What was the reaction of your congregation to this communion service?"

Rex replied, "Jude and Judy have really been my right-hand helpers at the church, and they're highly regarded for the work that they do for the church. Most of the people thought that it was a good idea to ask Jude to lead the service."

"Well," said Bishop Leiter, "some people told me that they were upset because Jude celebrated 'mass' at the church." Rex responded, "I would guess that you have been talking with Ira and Irene Petit. If so, I'm not surprised, since they have not been completely happy to see the Petitville church grow. In the good old days, they were the pillars of the church — nothing happened without their approval."

Bishop Leiter nodded his head, so Rex continued, "While most of the 'old-timers' have been happy to see the membership of the church increase, Ira and Irene seem a bit resentful at seeing their influence ebb away. They always had the ear of the previous pastor, while I try to consult as many people as possible, both old-timers and newcomers."

"The plot thickens," observed the bishop. "Are you saying that Ira and Irene resent the fact that Jude and Judy are now more prominent than they are?"

"I suppose you could say that," said Rex, "but how did you know?"

1. See the response of the United Methodist Church in *Churches Respond to BEM*, vol. II (Geneva: World Council of Churches, 1986), p. 188.

Bishop Leiter laughed for the first time during their meeting. "How do you think I got to be a bishop?"

As they shook hands, the bishop remarked, "After I've had a chance to talk with a couple people, I will get in touch. Meanwhile, don't get sick again."

A Theological Consultation

As soon as Rex had left, Bishop Leiter telephoned one of his seminary classmates, Zachary Zeigen, who was now a professor at their alma mater. "Zach, what's the difference between a 'mass' and 'a communion service'?"

Zachary replied, "Well Leo, that depends on what you have in mind. There can be a world of difference or no difference at all."

"Spoken like a true theologian, but no help to a busy bishop," teased Leo.

Zachary then explained that the celebration of the eucharist had different names in different traditions. "Protestants tend to call it 'a communion service,' Catholics use the term 'mass,' Orthodox use the term 'divine liturgy,' and so on, but all churches are basically celebrating what Jesus did at the Last Supper; in that sense, there's a difference in terminology, but not a difference in intention."

"Then there's only a difference in words?" asked Leo.

"Behind the words, there can be enormous differences in theology," Zach replied. "For example, Protestants and Catholics look upon the eucharist in quite different ways. Protestants ordinarily think of Jesus as being spiritually present at a communion service, while Catholics believe that Jesus is really present under the bread and wine. One obvious effect of this difference in theologies is that Catholics preserve the leftover 'consecrated bread and wine' while Protestants generally do not."

"But what about communion in the Methodist tradition?" asked Leo.

Zachary replied, "The Wesleys had the highest respect for

eucharistic worship and expounded in sermons and hymns a substantial eucharistic theology. In America, however, during a century and a half after John Wesley's death in 1791, the place of the holy communion in Methodist worship declined, and the beliefs about it lost continuity with the traditional doctrines which the Wesleys espoused."[2]

"Does that mean that United Methodist churches should celebrate communion more frequently?"

Zachary replied, "In United Methodism during recent years, a remarkable recovery of this tradition has been joined with the vigorous renewal of liturgical theology and practice in the ecumenical movement."[3]

"Are you saying my theology could use some updating?" asked the bishop.

"Well, it just happens that I am teaching a course on the eucharist this semester — would you like to attend?"

"How would it be if I took you to lunch instead? Then you could give me a crash course."

"Great," said Zachary. "I never pass up the chance to dine with a bishop. Why don't you come to chapel next Wednesday at eleven? That's when the seminary celebrates its weekly eucharist."

An Administrative Discussion

Later that week, Bishop Leiter met with Reverend Henry Herrisch, Rex's district superintendent. Leiter asked Herrisch, "What do you think should be done about the 'mass' at Petitville?" Herrisch replied, "I was hoping to ignore it."

Leo laughed, "That doesn't sound like you; you usually like to leap into problems."

"I only dive where the water is clear," Henry replied. "In this case it's hard to see where one would be leaping."

"What do you mean?" asked Leo.

2. *Churches Respond to BEM,* vol. II, p. 187.
3. Ibid.

Henry continued, "From a pastoral point of view, Rex is doing a good job. Petitville is a growing church; indeed, in terms of percentages, it's the fastest growing church in the district."

"But what about that former Roman Catholic priest?" asked the bishop.

Henry replied, "I can understand why some old-timers in the church got upset; Petitville has never been known for its ecumenical outreach. For generations, Roman Catholics weren't welcome there. And if some of the folks at Petitville were upset, I suspect that this incident could create some tension in our ecumenical relationship with the Roman Catholic clergy in the local council of churches."

Henry continued, "Yet, on the whole, I think Jude might make a good Methodist minister!"

"Are you serious?" asked the bishop.

Henry replied, "First of all, Rex told me about Jude's background some time ago. I told Rex, 'Let's see how things work out,' and in general, I've been pleased with the ministry that Jude has exercised. I didn't anticipate that Jude would celebrate the eucharist, but now that he has, perhaps we should make it official."

"Official?" asked the bishop. "That would be highly unusual."

"Well," replied the superintendent, "it's really no more unusual than allowing unordained pastors to preside at holy communion as we do in some of our small churches."[4]

"But that's different," protested the bishop.

"Isn't it more like six of one and half a dozen of the other?" asked the superintendent. "On the one hand, such pastors are officially licensed but lack ordination and have only a minimal theological education. In Jude's case, he has both a theological education and ordination but is not licensed as a Methodist pastor — or at least not yet."

"Are you suggesting that we should license Jude as a Methodist minister?"

4. Cf. *Churches Respond to BEM*, vol. II, p. 192.

Henry grinned. "Far be it from me to tell a bishop what to do."

POSSIBLE OUTCOMES

1. Bishop Leiter decided to act on the advice of Rex's district superintendent. Jude was officially licensed as a co-pastor at Petitville Church. The bishop also made arrangements through Professor Zeigen for Jude to take the seminary courses required for admission to full membership as a minister in the annual conference.

After the public announcement of these arrangements, Rex and Jude noticed the Petit's absence from church; it was later learned that Ira and Irene Petit and a few of their close friends were attending the small church at Kleindorf, some eight miles away. For several months, the collection was down, but it gradually climbed back to where it had been as new members registered in the church. Indeed, it looked like it was time to think of enlarging the church building.

2. Bishop Leiter made Rex and Jude an offer that they couldn't refuse. "I hope that neither of you has tied your heart to Petitville." After congratulating them on the good work that they had done and that he hoped that they would continue to do, he asked them to consider moving as a team to serve in a suburban church near the seminary.

"I want Rex to be the pastor, and I hope that you, Jude, would serve as a diaconal minister. You might also want to take some courses at the seminary that would qualify you for admission to the annual conference as a minister."

Rex knew that he had no choice but to accept the offer. Jude and Judy decided to attend services at Rex's new church but without their former involvement. A few months later, Jude and Judy moved to another part of the country.

3. When new assignments were announced that spring, Rex discovered that he had been reassigned to a pastorate in

a medium-sized church, some 150 miles from Petitville. Rex broke the news to Jude: "I've been kicked upstairs."

Rex's successor at Petitville was also a second-career minister, but there the resemblance ended. The new pastor, who had grown up in the area, soon made it abundantly clear to Jude and Judy that his plans for the church did not include them.

Several months later, when Bishop Leiter visited Petitville, he found that the congregation consisted mainly of "old-timers" like the Petits. When he asked the new pastor about attendance, he learned that most of the newcomers to the village now attended a recently established community church. The bishop asked, "And what happened to Jude and Judy Weihen?" The new pastor replied, "They're deacons at Petitville Community Church."

CASE STUDIES ON MINISTRY

9

Reception and Women's Ordination: An Anglican Experience in Southern Africa

(Anglican)

JULIA GATTA

It is no secret that the ordination of women is one of the most passionately debated issues in the ecumenical movement today. Commenting on this source of division among the churches, *Baptism, Eucharist and Ministry* notes the different theological convictions that animate each side of the dispute, while recommending that the "practical and theological questions within the various churches and Christian traditions should be complemented by joint study and reflection within the ecumenical fellowship of all churches."[1]

But the ordination of women is not only a matter of controversy among our churches: it also divides them from within. This is particularly true in the Anglican Communion, which is wrestling with the tensions that have emerged over the past twenty years as some Anglican churches have proceeded to ordain women as bishops, priests, or deacons, while others have not. Since 1970 the Episcopal Church in the United States has ordained women deacons, and in 1976 the General Convention of the Episcopal Church passed

---

1. See "Ministry," commentary on par. 18 in *Baptism, Eucharist and Ministry*.

legislation to permit the ordination of women to all orders. About the same time other Anglican synods — in Hong Kong, Canada, and New Zealand, for instance — also authorized the ordination of women to the priesthood; and since then Ireland and some dioceses in Africa have added women to their number of priests.

However, the priestly ministry of women ordained in these countries may not be exercised in Anglican provinces that do not ordain women: England, Wales, Australia, and most of Africa, South America, and the Far East. This strange situation, with its troubling practical consequences in which male priests are recognized abroad while female priests sometimes are not, has disturbed the very notion of an Anglican "Communion."

In the past, one of the hallmarks of "communion" within the Anglican Communion has always been the complete interchangeability of ordained ministries. This is no longer the rule within Anglicanism as a whole. Looked at from one angle, our communion with one another has suffered diminishment. But from another perspective, our common life has been enormously enriched. For with regard to the ordination of women, the Anglican Communion is undergoing "reception" — the spiritual process by which the Church, under the guidance of the Holy Spirit, comes to a common mind.[2] Until the ordination of women is fully accepted, we will be involved in this expansive, if arduous, process. This makes intra-Anglican relations something of a test case for the reception of women's ordination in the larger Christian world.

The Archbishop of Canterbury's Commission on Communion and Women in the Episcopate, to which I was recently

2. See, for example, the speech of Mary Tanner to the House of Bishops of the Episcopal Church (USA), September 23, 1989 (*Episcopal News Service*). An excellent introduction to the notion of reception may be found in William G. Rusch, *Reception: An Ecumenical Opportunity* (Philadelphia: Fortress Press with the Lutheran World Federation, 1988).

appointed, has called for a "genuinely open process of reception" in the church. At the same time, it candidly acknowledges "anomalies" that are bound to exist while the church undergoes this awkward period of testing a new phenomenon. In the meantime, Anglicans need to search for ways of deepening the "highest possible degree of communion" *(koinonia)* that already exists among them.[3]

In 1987, I experienced all these elements in contemporary Anglicanism firsthand: its ministerial "anomalies"; a willingness to explore the deep, if restricted, communion among Anglicans under different ecclesiastical disciplines; and a positive, though necessarily incomplete, reception of ministry from an ordained woman. That year, as a priest of the Episcopal Church in the United States, I was invited to teach for a term in a seminary of the church in the Province of Southern Africa, where women are not ordained to priesthood. My months at St. Bede's Theological College in Umtata, Transkei, have left me enormously hopeful not only about the reception of women's ordination but also about the prospects for unity in the church when we meet one another with respect, courtesy, and openheartedness.

I was initially asked to come to Southern Africa in order to give the seminarians, and others whom I would meet, some exposure to an Anglican priest who happened to be female. Since the question of women's ordination to the priesthood had been debated in the Anglican synod there for some years, it was felt that the issue remained unrealistically abstract so long as Anglicans in South Africa had little contact with women priests from other parts of the Communion. (The church in Southern Africa had just begun ordaining women to the diaconate when I arrived, but these deacons were few in number.) Simply by inviting me to come, my South African hosts had taken a first step in that "open process of reception"

3. *Report of the Archbishop of Canterbury's Commission on Communion and Women in the Episcopate 1989* (Anglican Consultative Council), par. 42, 51–53; pp. 20, 22–23.

commended by the Archbishop's Commission. They were prepared to welcome a woman priest from another church of the Anglican Communion with genuine hospitality and a readiness to listen.

I realized on my part that while in South Africa I would not be permitted to celebrate the eucharist or administer the other sacraments. Naturally, I felt this privation as a keen loss, for like any other priest, I find unfailing joy in the exercise of the sacramental ministry. However, I was acutely aware of my ordination promises to obey the discipline of the church and those in authority over me. To have engaged in any surreptitious or defiant celebrations would have involved me in a flat self-contradiction and would, I believe, have undermined the meaning of the great sacrament of unity itself. Foregoing for a while the exercise of a sacramental ministry was an anomaly I could bear for the sake of unity. As it turned out, this restriction actually helped further the acceptance of women in priesthood in Southern Africa.

With the other faculty, lay and ordained, and with the students, I attended daily worship in the seminary chapel. I took my turn preaching and leading the daily office. I participated as communicant each day at the eucharist. In a parish church in Cape Town, where I was invited to preach, I also read the Gospel and administered the chalice. On these occasions when I performed functions normally assigned to a deacon or assisting priest, I vested as a priest. My hosts and I were committed to ecclesiastical obedience, yet I was encouraged to manifest the "highest possible degree of communion" with them as a fellow Anglican and sister in ministry. As I prayed with my students and colleagues day after day at the seminary, we did indeed experience our unity and communion as God's gift, which no disparity in discipline could undo.

Shortly after I arrived at St. Bede's, I learned that a straw vote had been taken the previous year on the question of women's ordination — and it had been roundly defeated! I realized at once the delicacy of my position. Yet I had not, in

98

any case, come to preach about myself. I was there to teach a course in Christian spirituality. I told my students at my first meeting with them that if anyone wished to discuss the ordination of women with me outside of class, I would gladly respond to their questions. There were many such conversations, but only after some degree of trust had been established. Meanwhile, I was almost glad for my enforced separation from the altar. Once the students realized that female ministrations were not about to be imposed on them, they grew considerably more at ease with me.

Since I usually wear a dark suit and clerical collar when engaged in the ministry of teaching, I continued my custom at St. Bede's. Then on Sundays I donned a cassock, as did all the students and the ordained members of the faculty. I could tell that my dress was quite an eye opener for everybody at first! Those powerful symbols of ordination incarnated something my fellow Anglicans had known previously only as a practice in some remote part of their Communion. After only a week or two, however, I no longer drew amazed stares from the seminary community. A woman in clerical clothes became a familiar sight for a while; I blended in with my ordained colleagues. The students could recognize the family resemblance between me and their priests back home, and they offered me the same respect and, in time, the same affection.

What probably brought us all together was the subject matter of my course: the practice of prayer and the disciplines of the spiritual life. This is not a subject that lends itself to posturing or superficiality. As we encountered one another at a very profound level of the Spirit, I was moved by the transparency with which these black South African men shared with a white woman from America their interior struggles and joys. Here, too, we felt how in Christ we enjoy a unity that transcends all social, political, ecclesial, and sexual divisions. And while we refrained from addressing women's ordination in the classroom, my students knew I spoke from experience when, at the appropriate point in the curriculum, I coached them on preparation for hearing confessions. I think we all felt the poignancy of these ministerial "anomalies" with particular force that day.

How, in retrospect, do I evaluate this particular experience of reception? Precisely because the Anglican Communion is committed to respecting the varying disciplinary practices among its provincial churches, reception could only be partial. Yet because we are also committed to seeking the "highest possible degree of communion" within the Communion that already exists, reception was nonetheless genuine and remarkably deep.

The very constraints under which the church labors in South Africa had a way of sharpening the issues for us. I heard of a telling incident shortly after my departure. It seems a number of indignant students approached the faculty and administration and wanted to know why they had not pressed the local bishop more urgently to let me celebrate the eucharist in the seminary chapel! But I could accept the reception I had been given and recognized how even the restrictions managed to open an issue which at that time in South Africa seemed still in an early phase of discussion. In addition, while I was in Cape Town, Archbishop Tutu offered me a wholly unsolicited apology for the constraints placed on me while in his province. Certainly he, if anyone, knows how to "bring forth fruit with patience" (Lk. 8:15).

DISCUSSION QUESTIONS

1. If you, as a woman priest, were invited to teach in a region of the Anglican Communion where you could not exercise your sacramental ministry, would you accept the invitation?

2. If you, as a woman priest, were visiting a region of the Anglican Communion where women are not ordained to the priesthood, would you celebrate the eucharist as a matter of conscientious protest?

3. Since the Anglican Communion allows for a diversity of practice

regarding the ordination of women among its provincial churches, in certain respects it is a microcosm of the ecumenical situation. How can this example of reception within Anglicanism serve as a model for the "joint study and reflection" on women's ordination that BEM has recommended take place "within the ecumenical fellowship of churches"? What aspects of the Anglican context are not transferable?

4. The *Report of the Archbishop of Canterbury's Commission on Communion and Women in the Episcopate* (Eames Commission) urged Anglican churches to foster the "highest possible degree of communion" *(koinonia)* among themselves even in strained circumstances. What were the deeper levels of communion discovered by Mother Gatta and her South African hosts? How did the sense of *koinonia* create a fruitful context for the discussion and reception of women's ordination?

5. What depth of communion — in the trinitarian life of God, in the mystical body of Christ, in baptism, eucharistic sharing, and common witness and ministry — is possible in our present ecumenical situation?

10

An Interdenominational Ministry?

(United Methodist/Presbyterian)

RENA YOCOM

Jill Rickman, a diaconal minister (permanent deacon) in the United Methodist Church, was offered employment as a director of Christian education at a local Presbyterian church. In accordance with United Methodist polity, she applied to her Annual Conference Board of Diaconal Ministry and to her resident bishop to approve this appointment "an ecumenical church-related assignment."[1] The Conference Board of Diaconal Ministry found that there were other precedents for this type of arrangement with other communions and gave their approval. The board forwarded their recommendation to the resident bishop; however, when the proposed appointment reached the episcopal office, the bishop refused to approve the employment of a diaconal minister in a local church of another denomination.

Jill and a representative from her conference board met with the bishop and pointed out that the United Methodist Discipline allowed "ecumenical assignments." They also noted other precedents of this nature in other jurisdictions,

1. *The Book of Discipline of the United Methodist Church* (Nashville: United Methodist Publishing House, 1984), par. 311.

102

including a musician who was employed by a Roman Catholic church. The bishop pointed out that the disciplinary provision allowing for ecumenical assignment ends with the phrase "in the field of service in which he/she is approved by the bishop." He believed that "ecumenical assignment" should only include agencies that were cooperatively formed by multiple denominations, such as the urban ministry network. In such a setting, United Methodists would have equal authority with any other denomination. Such a situation would not exist in the local church of another denomination because a United Methodist bishop has no authority in the local church of any other denomination, and no other denominational official has any authority in a local United Methodist church. Further, no valid assignment should keep a United Methodist from working and worshiping regularly with other United Methodists.

The board representative pointed out how difficult this situation would be for Jill if her appointment were not approved. She would be forced to take a leave of absence until she could find employment with a United Methodist congregation. Without employment she would obviously be without income and without benefits, such as insurance and pension. Unlike the elder in the United Methodist Church, there is no guaranteed appointment for the diaconal minister.

Since the bishop did not want to make it unnecessarily difficult for Jill and since another bishop had made a different judgment, he did agree to pursue the question.

At a meeting of the Council of Bishops, another bishop facing a similar decision approved the appointment because he interpreted the role of episcopal jurisdiction as related to the person, i.e., how the individual fulfilled the office of deacon, and not the employment setting, per se. Because there was no disciplinary clarity, the case could be referred to the judicial council. Does (or under what condition does) a bishop have the authority to appoint a person to a local church of another denomination?

DISCUSSION QUESTIONS

1. If you were the chair of the Conference Board of Diaconal Ministry, what advice would you give to Jill? What would you say to the bishop?

2. If you were on the Judicial Council, what decision would you make? What are the reasons for your decision?

3. If you were Jill's bishop, would you approve her service appointment? Why or why not? Does it make any difference that it is a Presbyterian congregation?

4. If you were Jill, what would you do?

COMMENTARY

1. If you were the chair of the Conference Board of Diaconal Ministry, what advice would you give to Jill? What would you say to the bishop?

At the time that Jill's situation surfaced, there were three other similar appointments that served as precedents. The chairperson obtained those names and places so that the bishop could be assured that he was not acting alone on this interpretation of "ecumenical assignment."

The chairperson also delineated the personal hardship that a refusal would place upon Jill. The possibility was raised that an "interim" approval might be given either to see how the situation might be lived out or to give Jill time to seek other employment.

This "interim" approval would assure Jill of income, insurance, and pension benefits during the interval in question. This "interim" approval would need to be a matter of "understanding" communicated by letter as there was no such category in the Discipline.

The chairpersons also advised Jill to consider the "leave

104

of absence" option that was available to her.[2] This would give her three years in which she could be employed anywhere, with or without the bishop's permission. This would give her time to find other employment in a United Methodist setting or ecumenical work that was cooperative rather than congregationally based.

Additionally, the chairperson contacted the national office and asked it to pursue the issue by defining "ecumenical assignment" so that an individual might not be quite so vulnerable to each bishop's interpretation. There was some hesitation from the national office to make this a public issue, however, lest they jeopardize the ecumenical appointment of some who were already approved.

2. If you were on the Judicial Council, what decision would you make? What are the reasons for your decision?

The Judicial Council operates as a constitutional jury or court. It has the authority "to determine the constitutionality of any act . . . to hear and determine any appeal from a bishop's decision . . . [and] all decisions of the Judicial Council shall be final."[3] In these matters, the council sustains or overturns the actions or decisions under consideration or finds that it stands beyond the matter of constitution and church law and renders no decision. The council is also authorized to make declaratory decisions as to the "constitutionality, meaning, application, or effect of the Discipline or any portion thereof . . . and the decision of the Judicial Council thereon shall be as binding. . . ."[4]

Since no decision has yet been made, this would be a declaratory decision. The council should first consider the section of the Discipline that treats the diaconal minister:

2. *The Book of Discipline*, par. 313.1.d.
3. The Constitution, Part I of *The Book of Discipline*, par. 58–61.
4. *The Book of Discipline*, par. 2615.

Service Appointment of Diaconal Ministers

Diaconal ministers may serve (a) within a local congregation or larger parish, (b) through church-related agencies, or (c) through other ministries which extend the witness and service of Christ's love and justice in the world through equipping persons to fulfill their own calls to Christian service.

Diaconal ministers serve in a non-itinerating ministry. A district superintendent or bishop may initiate or recommend an appointment, but they have no responsibility to do so.

The service appointment of the diaconal minister shall be (a) initiated by the individual diaconal minister or agency seeking his/her service; (b) clarified by a written statement of intentionality of diakonia . . . ; (c) recommended by the Conference Board of Diaconal Ministry; (d) reviewed by the Cabinet and approved by the bishop of the Annual Conference.

Service of Diaconal Ministers

Service must be in a local congregation or larger parish, an agency of The United Methodist Church, an ecumenical church-related assignment, or a ministry which extends the witness and service of Christ's love and justice in the world through equipping persons to fulfill their own calls to Christian service . . . the work of ministry in the field of service in which he/she is approved by the bishop.

Change in Conference Relationship

Diaconal ministers seeking a change in conference relationship shall make written request to their Conference Board stating the reasons for the requested change in status.

Personal leave

When a diaconal minister is temporarily unable or unwilling to perform the work of his/her ministry, a personal leave of absence may be granted upon recommendation of the Conference Board of Diaconal Ministry. This relation shall be approved annually and shall not be granted for more than three consecutive years.[5]

The council should also consider the chapter concerning the duties of the bishop (general superintendent):

1. To make and fix the appointments in the Annual Conference . . . as the Discipline may direct.

2. To divide or to unite a circuit(s), station(s), or mission(s) as judged necessary for missional strategy and then to make appropriate appointments.

3. To read the appointments of deaconesses, diaconal ministers . . . and home missionaries.

Pastors and clergy in appointments beyond the local church shall be appointed by a bishop, who is empowered to make and fix all appointments in the episcopal area within which the Annual Conference is a part. Appointments are to be made with consideration of the gifts and graces of those appointed, to the needs, characteristics, and opportunities of congregations and institutions. . . . Through appointment making, the connectional nature of the United Methodist system is made visible.[6]

The council should survey the constitution to see if there were any related issues. In this issue of diaconal ministry (per-

5. *The Book of Discipline,* par. 310, 311, 313.1d.
6. Ibid., par. 516 and 529.

manent deacons) there are none. The constitution simply states that "the bishops shall appoint, after consultation with the district superintendents, ministers to the charges; and they shall have such responsibilities and authorities as the General Conference shall prescribe."[7]

The council should survey previous council decisions to see if any applied to this situation. In 1970, the council ruled that an annual conference has no authority to change the provisions of the Discipline. At that time they ruled that "a procedure which would compel a conference member seeking special appointment to a non-United Methodist agency to change his conference status to sabbatical leave or voluntary location . . . does make such changes and is, therefore, unconstitutional."[8]

To make this ruling applicable, one would need to ask if "non-United Methodist agency" and "non-United Methodist local church" can be equated.

3. If you were Jill's bishop, would you approve her service appointment? Why or why not? Does it make any difference that it is a Presbyterian congregation?

When Jill's bishop consulted with others in the council of bishops, he found a variety of opinions. Some rejoiced at any work that was done with "sister" churches. Some believed that if they had no alternative appointment possibility, it was unfair to "punish" her because she found employment with another communion. More than one bishop used this as a reason why the church should resist this "whole business" of permanent deacons. Another expressed this as a test case regarding the appointment-making powers of the bishop. One brave bishop believed that (especially since the other denomination was Presbyterian) the recognition of ministerial orders by the Consultation on Church Union would include recognition of ministry within that denomination. One bishop

7. The Constitution, par. 57.
8. Decision #325.

108

expressed a belief that the issue was not the authority of the bishop over the setting for ministry but the role of the bishop in assuring the church that the setting was one in which the individual could fulfill her diaconal commitment.

4. If you were Jill, what would you do?

Jill reviewed the decisions she had made for her life. She knew God had called her to ministry. The permanent diaconate seemed very right. She reread the disciplinary passage:

> Very early in its history the Church instituted an order of ordained ministers to personify or focus the servanthood to which all Christians are called. These people were named deacons. Those who are called to this representative ministry of service in the Church and world may be set apart to the office of diaconal minister. This ministry exemplifies the servanthood every Christian is called to live in both Church and world. . . .[9]

She reread the statements from the Consultation on Church Union:

> The deacon is the People's helper or servant. . . . To the deacon is assigned a special role in the Church's ministry of teaching, in its assistance to those in need of any sort. . . .[10]

She recalled her consecration. When the bishop had imposed hands he had said to her, "Take the ministries of love, justice, and service." She knew that, unlike the elders, there was no guarantee of an appointment in the Methodist Church; she also knew that she would have some say in where she served.

What would she do if the bishop refused her appoint-

9. *Book of Discipline*, par. 302.
10. Gerald F. Moede, ed., *The COCU Consensus: In Quest of a Church of Christ Uniting* (Princeton, N.J.: Consultation on Church Union, 1985), p. 53.

ment? She was not sure how eagerly she could serve if she did not have full approval from her own denomination. Could she transfer to another conference where she knew the bishop had approved such an ecumenical assignment? (The viability of that option dwindled when she learned that a diaconal minister needs to live within the bounds of the conference of appointment.) If she wanted to become a Presbyterian, the pastor who wanted to hire her had offered to recommend her to the presbytery. She had a master of divinity degree. If she were to be an elder, she could pursue that in her own tradition (and then be guaranteed an appointment). Had she been unrealistic in believing that such an ecumenical assignment was justifiable? How should she handle her feelings about this whole episode?

POSSIBLE OUTCOMES

1. The Judicial Council ruled that there was no provision in the United Methodist Constitution that gave a bishop authority to appoint a person to a local congregation of another denomination. The bishop interpreted the ruling of the Judicial Council to mean that he could not under any circumstances approve Jill's appointment as requested. Jill was forced to accept a "personal leave" until she could find an "acceptable place of employment." Jill used part of her free time to network with others to get a more understanding bishop at the end of the quadrennium (only two years away.)

2. The bishop did not feel the need to send the question to the Judicial Council; he simply refused to appoint Jill to the requested employment. She was disillusioned, anxious, and out of work. Although the permanent diaconate had seemed "right" for her, she decided to be "realistic" instead. She applied for candidacy into the sacramental ministry and asked the bishop and cabinet to appoint her to a charge.

3. As Jill's bishop discussed Jill's request with other bishops, he realized that the essential question was whether or

not Jill could serve the Church of Jesus Christ in a way faithful to her own calling. He further realized that Jill would be in a strategic place to model what it could mean to take the COCU covenant seriously. He might even have his conference communicator write a feature article and mail it to the appropriate bodies.

4. With many misgivings about setting precedents, Jill's bishop approved her appointment based on the previous Judicial Council ruling #325. Jill, wanting to be faithful to her own denominational polity, thanked the bishop and promised to begin looking for other employment. The chairperson of the Conference Board of Diaconal Ministry sent a request to the current Commission to Study the Ministry to take the issue under advisement and incorporate an answer in the next General Conference Report.

11

A Black Minister
for a White Congregation

(United Methodist)

NEHEMIAH THOMPSON

Chettoor, New York, is a small village of three hundred people. Its population consists of 50 percent farmers, 30 percent workers in various industries, and 20 percent professionals. The membership of the United Methodist Church of Chettoor, the only church in the village, can be broken down by the same proportions. While the United Methodist Church of Chettoor is socially conservative, it is theologically moderate: the congregation accepted a woman minister at a time when women ministers were not accepted in churches of this nature, and she exercised a successful ministry there for some time. The all-white church, however, had never had a black minister. The African-Americans living in Chettoor attend a Baptist church ten miles away.

After eight years of service, the woman minister requested a transfer and moved to another church. At the time, there was a tremendous shortage of ministers in that conference. The district superintendent tried his best to recruit a student minister from the nearby seminary for the congregation but was unsuccessful. Finally, he ended up recruiting the Reverend Peter Shawat, an African-American in his late twenties, who was willing to take that parish.

The district superintendent took Peter to be interviewed by the Pastor-Parish Relations Committee, but before the interview he met privately with the PPR Committee to let them know that the minister they would be interviewing was black. The superintendent's proposal met with unanimous disapproval and even anger among the committee members. Warning the committee that no one else was available, the superintendent suggested that the church either go without a minister for another year or accept Peter. He even preached inclusiveness and Christian brotherhood regardless of skin color. After a three-hour discussion, the committee, by a four to three vote, decided to accept Peter for a three-month trial period.

The following Sunday the all-white congregation gathered. Peter delivered one of his best sermons — and one of the best sermons the congregation had heard as well. He found widespread acceptance in the congregation but not among all the members. Surprisingly, the educated, white-collar members were more resentful of Peter than the less educated, blue-collar members, but they didn't have enough support among the other members to reject Peter simply because he was not white. The Pastor–Parish Relations Committee met again and, by a four to three vote, invited the minister to move in with his family.

Peter delivered great sermons Sunday after Sunday, and his approval rate rose steadily. He was dedicated to his pastoral duties as well: he visited the sick and the elderly regularly and gave deeply moving sermons at funeral services.

One prominent member of the church, an executive of the local baby food firm, best expressed the prevailing attitude of the church members when he said, "I love his sermons, but he is black." Some members postponed their children's baptisms until a white minister would come, probably the following year, but the same people loved Peter's preaching. Some people invited a former minister or a minister whom their friend's friends knew to conduct their children's weddings, but they still liked Peter's sermons. Peter did not have to allow these outside ministers to officiate, but he did so out of the goodness of his heart.

Peter was aware of what was going on. He recalled that the United Methodist *Book of Resolutions* condemns racism in no uncertain terms, prohibiting the practice of excluding Asian, Black, Hispanic and Native American clergy from full and total participation in the appointment process of the itinerant ministry. It declares that "the house of God must be open to the whole family of God. If we discriminate against any persons, we deny the essential nature of the church as a fellowship in Christ." It calls upon all district superintendents and bishops "to encourage *open pulpits* and integrate cabinets, and to appoint pastors to churches and charges without respect to the racial opposition of the congregations or the race of the appointed minister."[1]

The Social Principles of the church also contain a strongly worded statement on racism and condemn racism as sin.[2] Finally, the Constitution of the church clearly states, "In the United Methodist Church no conference or other organizational unit of the church shall be structured so as to exclude any member or any constituent body of the church because of race, color, national origin, or economic condition."[3]

Peter wondered why these teachings had not reached the local church and why people of his church were so obviously divided on this issue. Why did this congregation go on ignoring the church's condemnation of racism?

Peter was equally concerned about the Consultation on Church Union in that the United Methodist Church was seeking visible unity with eight other denominations, including three historic black churches. COCU envisions that in order for the church to be a "Church of Christ Uniting" as

1. *Book of Resolutions of the United Methodist Church* (Nashville: United Methodist Publishing House, 1988), pp. 207, 301–302.

2. Ibid., 21.

3. *The Book of Discipline of the United Methodist Church* (Nashville: United Methodist Publishing House, 1984), p. 20.

"a community of hope and love, it must also find means for healing the divisions among people who are alienated as a result of such unChristian attitudes as racism, sexism, ageism and handicapism."[4] Peter did not see the healing of divisions in this situation. COCU further declares that the Uniting Church's "racial and ethnic multiplicity will be held forth both as one of its richest gifts and the most persuasive witness that the reconciliation it offers to the world in the name of Christ is already at work in its midst." Peter could not see this reconciliation at work in the United Methodist Church at Chettoor.

The year ended. The time had come for the PPR committee to make its recommendation to the district superintendent. Once again by a majority vote (this time, five to two) the committee asked the minister to stay another year, knowing that moving the good preacher would split the congregation. The angry chairperson of the PPR committee resigned and began attending the local Reformed church, whose minister didn't see the rationale of "imposing" a black minister on a white congregation. Peter stayed with his church for five years and then moved to another all-white church on his own initiative.

In the meantime, the Chettoor United Methodist Church became a star in the conference for "accepting" a black minister. A conference lay leader, who proposed to recognize that church for its "courageous witness," commented in an interview published in the conference newsletter that his local all-white church was "not ready" for a black minister and admired Chettoor for its courage.

DISCUSSION QUESTIONS

1. How would you have voted at the last meeting of the PPR committee? Why?

4. *COCU Consensus,* p. 10.

2. If you were Peter, would you have accepted the position at Chettoor?

3. If you were a member of Chettoor United Methodist Church, would you invite a former minister or your friend's minister to conduct your wedding?

4. By accepting the invitation to baptize or to solemnize weddings in that church, do you think the guest ministers approved the racism of some of the members of that congregation?

5. Do you think the statement of the Conference lay leader is honest or hypocritical?

6. How do you understand racial and ethnic inclusiveness and how does this situation in Chettoor fit into your understanding of inclusiveness?

7. Why do you think there is disparity between the *Book of Resolutions* and the life of the church?

8. Do you think COCU is too idealistic in promoting racial and ethnic inclusivity? Do you think racism can be eradicated?

12

A Woman Pastor at Potter's Falls?

(United Church of Christ)

GAIL M. REYNOLDS

Background Note

The United Church of Christ, through its predecessor denomination, the Congregational Church, has ordained
women to Christian ministry since 1853 when Antoinette
Brown, a graduate of Oberlin Theological School, was ordained in the Congregational Church in South Butler, New
York. At present there are 1,616 ordained women in the
denomination, 535 of whom serve local churches. Also, the
congregational polity of the United Church of Christ specifies that each local church has the freedom and the responsibility to choose its pastoral leadership under the guidance
of the Holy Spirit. Judicatory leaders such as the conference
minister have the function of identifying possible candidates
to local churches and assisting them in the search process.

The pulpit of Prince of Peace United Church of Christ in
Potter's Falls is open. The search committee has been formed
and has done a self-study to determine what skills and talents
the next minister needs to have in order to lead the church
in the next decade. Ministers from around the country, both

male and female, have applied for the position. After four months of considering résumés, the search committee invites the conference minister to meet with them to assist them in breaking a deadlock. The committee cannot even agree upon whom it ought to invite for an interview.

At the opening of the meeting, the conference minister asks if the committee has been using other criteria by which to evaluate their candidates than the ones listed in the self-study. The question meets with silence. "Have you tallied the skills of the applicants and matched them with your list?"

Finally, one of the women committee members mumbles, "Yes."

"And what was the result?"

The chair of the committee pushes a piece of paper down the table. On the sheet are the names of applicants ranked according to how congruent their skills are with the church's expressed needs. Number one is the Reverend Harriet Morse. Number two is the Reverend Genevieve Long. Following in a distant third is the Reverend Bill McLeod.

"Tell me what your response to Harriet Morse is as you consider her candidacy," suggests the conference minister.

Harry Smith quickly says, "She's obviously the best qualified for our position. She has great references and has done an excellent job in her most recent parish, but they don't want to interview her."

A younger man rubs his hands together and drawls, "Yeah, Harry's right about her being hands-down the best qualified, but I don't know. It's risky to call a woman. I'm afraid they won't go for her."

"Who is 'they'?" asks the conference minister.

"I don't know how a woman preacher will go over with the womenfolk," explains the speaker. "I just think they would be opposed."

The woman to his left chimes in, "I'll tell you right now, Ron Tyler, they won't vote for her! Why, do you realize, she isn't married? What if she gets here and one of our men gets sweet on her? She could break up a happy marriage! No woman in this congregation is going to want a single, pretty, young woman presenting that kind of temptation in the pulpit."

A younger woman at the end of the table jerks her chair closer to the table. "Doris, you don't speak for all the women in this church. We don't know enough about Harriet Morse to come to any of the conclusions you've drawn. I'd like to see her in person, have a chance to talk with her, evaluate how she'd fit in here in Potter's Falls. I think we owe her that much consideration and ourselves that much curiosity."

Dr. Morgan, the committee chair, interrupts. "Don't forget it's going to cost us a fortune to fly her in here from Wyoming for an interview. Bill McLeod is just a hundred miles away. I think we ought to interview him. He's not bad on paper. And you know, men have always been the pastors here. It might be too much for this Reverend Morse to buck the tradition. She probably wouldn't like it here anyway."

Here Harry explodes and pounds the table. "I won't settle for somebody who is just 'not bad'! Bill McLeod only rates fourteen points on our list of criteria. Harriet Morse scores fifty-six! I've been in business long enough to know that you pay in the long run if you settle for second best, and Bill McLeod is not even second best by our own tabulations. We owe it to ourselves and to the church to interview the very best candidates we can find for this position. Harriet Morse is obviously competent, and I think she has the right to decide whether or not she could be happy here. You're just afraid of new possibilities, Sam Morgan."

A middle-aged woman, Sarah Townley, nods her head. "Yes, at some point we have to put personal biases aside and look at who is qualified to serve us — male or female. The issue is, Who can do the job? I know as a CPA I've always felt I've had to prove myself because I'm a woman. I don't think it's fair to dismiss the possibility of interviewing a well-qualified person on the basis of gender."

Dr. Morgan heaves a huge sigh. Turning to the conference

minister, he throws up his hands. "You see. We're hopelessly deadlocked. Three of us don't think it's worth the time and money to call in Reverend Morse for an interview. The other three keep pressuring us to do it. What are we going to do?"

DISCUSSION QUESTIONS

1. If you were a member of the search committee, how would you have voted? Why?

2. What are the underlying issues and fears of the deadlocked committee?

3. Which of these are theological issues? Which are sociological in nature? To what extent is Doris's rejection of Harriet Morse's candidacy based upon theological or sociological factors? Are there other factors at work? What about Dr. Morgan's rejection of Reverend Morse? Or Ron Tyler's?

4. Given the congregational polity of the denomination, what kind of leadership could the conference minister have given previously to prepare Prince of Peace UCC in Potter's Falls for receiving a woman minister?

5. In what ways are women in ministry an issue in your church? Which factors are theological? Which factors are sociological?

POSSIBLE OUTCOMES

Suppose you are the conference minister. What options are there to address the problem at Prince of Peace UCC in Potter's Falls, given the present situation? Consider the merits and drawbacks of the following options:

1. You recommend that before the committee considers interviewing anyone, they have a "mock" interview with a woman pastor nearby to hone their questions and to prepare

themselves for the questions a candidate might ask of them but also to experience a woman in ministry.

2. You offer to invite a competent woman minister to fill the pulpit at Prince of Peace UCC on an interim basis so that they can both experience a woman minister's leadership in worship and get to know one on a more personal basis for a limited period of time. You suggest that they put their search on hold for a two-month period.

3. You remind the committee of the constitution and bylaws of the United Church of Christ and of subsequent resolutions of the denomination's general synods that assert that all baptized members of the church have the right to be considered for ordination to Christian ministry in the church, regardless of gender. You insist that as an ordained minister in the United Church of Christ, Harriet Morse has a right to be given the opportunity to interview with them.

4. You recommend that the committee start its search from scratch, setting aside its present candidates and that in the new search, all names and indications of gender be erased from resumes. Ask the committee members to covenant together at the beginning that whoever emerges as the candidate with the best credentials will be interviewed regardless of gender.

5. You recommend that the committee look again at the Reverend Genevieve Long's résumé, knowing that the Reverend Long has a husband and a teenage daughter. You think, in so doing, that some of Doris's objections may be met and that Genevieve Long may be a compromise candidate.

6. You decide that Potter's Falls UCC is not ready for a woman as its pastor and reluctantly agree that the committee should interview Bill McLeod, promising yourself and them that you will work on the issue of a woman pastor for the future

7. Can you think of other options?

ECUMENICAL REFLECTIONS

13

Reception of Ecumenism: A Theological Rationale

EMMANUEL SULLIVAN

Few Christians have difficulty subscribing to the ideal and vision of Christian unity expressed in the prayer of Christ "that all may be one . . . that the world may believe" (Jn. 17:21). The problem for the churches in our time is how to translate the ideal to the real; how to respond practically to the vision given.

This essay presents one such view, that of a Roman Catholic ecumenist, who hopes that this vision will be shared by the wider ecumenical community. In the early days of the ecumenical movement in this century, great emphasis was placed on seeking more visible unity among the churches, for how could Christians expect to give a credible witness to non-Christians if those who preached the Gospel were divided over its meaning?

Even in Christian countries, the churches' efforts at witness and service sometimes gave the wrong impression. For example, in the minds of many, the image of the churches sometimes resembled that of corporations competing in the business of "winning souls for Christ" and increasing congregational membership. However, after World War II, there was a definite shift as churches began to perceive their own need for spiritual renewal and change within themselves.

One notable example is the Second Vatican Council, which brought the Roman Catholic Church into the mainstream of the ecumenical movement. While the main effort of the Council was renewal within Roman Catholicism, such efforts served to encourage other churches to accelerate the renewal already occurring within their own church life. Renewal became important for ecumenism.

The Second Vatican Council also prompted an unexpected enthusiasm for ecumenism. Ecumenical attitudes took a quantum leap. Polemical attitudes began to disappear and interchurch cooperation became commonplace. Parish clergy and laity began to wonder where ecumenism was leading: Did ecumenism mean simply that a new plateau of tolerance and Christian solidarity had been reached?

Practical pastoral questions surfaced on issues such as "ecumenical marriages" and eucharistic intercommunion: What is the future of Christian unity? Is it realistic to expect Christian churches to unite in one visible community of faith?

While such discussions were occurring on the local level, formal dialogues were taking place at the national and international levels between theologians officially appointed by their churches to discuss church-dividing issues. These bilateral and multilateral dialogues have been remarkably successful in reducing tensions among Christians over doctrinal matters. They have shown where the differences are real and where they are far less divisive than history and culture made them seem. In some instances churches have been able to see their doctrinal positions converging or even being in substantial agreement.

Given the ecumenical agreements on the theological level, Christians frequently ask, What is the impact of these agreements about faith on the pastoral life of local congregations? How are these agreements being *received* by the churches? Thus, a fourth term has been introduced into the theology of the ecumenical movement — *reception*.

The ecumenical movement now has to deal with all four components, namely, unity, mission, renewal, and reception.

All four belong together if the ecumenical movement is to lead anywhere and establish its credibility and reality in the bloodstream of our churches' life together. Otherwise we are on a journey leading nowhere, an endless voyage without a port of call. Precisely because our destiny as churches is full, visible communion, we have to think and talk about the factor of reception.

While the term "reception" may sound new, in theological discussions, in fact, the Christian church throughout its history has always had to deal with the phenomenon of reception. First of all, faith itself is a gift from God that has to be received. The church's faith is received through a careful receiving of God's word in the Scriptures and an entering into the mystery of God through participation in the life and worship of the church: the church is where "the Gospel is taught purely and the sacraments are administered rightly."[1] In other words, reception is at the very root of our Christian faith.

We need a spirit of openness, a spirit of receptivity to the new life God offers us and our churches. In speaking of reception, we necessarily have to speak of the Holy Spirit.

The Spirit of God creates the right kind of openness and receptivity the churches need. Such reception makes us responsible for "handing on" what we have received (Col. 2:6; 1 Cor. 15:1; Gal. 1:9–12; 1 Cor. 11:23). We call this faith that we have received and that we are called to pass on to others *the apostolic faith.*

The apostolic faith is not a religious ideology conceived and propagated by a privileged hierarchy. Nor is the apostolic faith received through a chain of command from a rigidly structured authority.[2] It is a faith received from God and handed on in the life of the church from age to age. The apostolic faith creates a sense of communion throughout the whole membership of the

---

1. See Preface in *Baptism, Eucharist and Ministry.*
2. See Roman Catholic/Lutheran Joint Commission, *Facing Unity: Models, Forms and Phases of Catholic-Lutheran Church Fellowship* (Geneva: Lutheran World Federation, 1985), pp. 16–17.

127

church. The task of communicating the apostolic faith is reflected in Acts 15, which describes how the decisions of that
first ecumenical council of Jerusalem were reached by "the
apostles and the elders, *with the whole church*" (v. 22).

ECUMENICAL RECEPTION

Reception may be used in two ways: the first classical, the
second ecumenical. In the *classical* sense, reception refers to the
process in the early church whereby the church attempted to
maintain a basic communion among all its members and among
all the local churches. When a question or controversy arose in
one place and the church there came to a decision, it was
communicated to the other churches throughout the ancient
world. In other words, the decisions of the church in one region
were communicated worldwide, so that such decisions could
be received by all other churches. This process of reception later
became associated with the so-called "ecumenical" councils,
whose decisions were regarded as normative for the church
throughout the world.

In its *ecumenical* sense, reception refers to the process
whereby the churches no longer in communion with one
another attempt through dialogue to find a consensus about
matters of faith and practice. Ecumenical dialogue is, of course,
a complex process; it usually begins with an attempt to understand what truly divides the churches and to discover what truly
unites them, where they differ and where they fundamentally
agree. Such a process has been at work since the publication of
Baptism, Eucharist and Ministry in 1982. Since that date,
churches throughout the world have studied and responded to
the question of "the extent to which your church can recognize
in this text the faith of the Church throughout the ages."[3]

3. Preface, BEM. For a useful survey of the meaning of reception,
see William Rusch, *Reception: An Ecumenical Opportunity* (Philadelphia: Fortress Press, 1987).

In receiving ecumenical consensus statements, it is worth remembering that in spite of the centuries of Christian division, the Holy Spirit has been at work in the churches through the ages. Unfortunately in the past, the differences among Christians were sources of division; the ecumenical movement seeks to discover the unity underlying such differences. Rather than regarding denominational differences as necessarily divisive, different denominational traditions can be seen as providing a rich heritage for the united church of the future.

The ecumenical movement seeks "a unity in reconciled diversity"[4] in which each denomination contributes the richness of its traditions. Thus, unity would unite the churches without one church absorbing another. Insofar as they are "sister churches," there would be a unifying family resemblance. Insofar as they are as different as sisters, the churches would respect what the Holy Spirit has done in their individual histories as separate denominations.

Any theological rationale has to take into account two dimensions in the process of reception. First, one must receive God's gifts to one's own denomination. Secondly and similarly, one must receive God's gifts to other denominations. This does not mean that everything that has happened in other denominations is of God, just as one can hardly credit God with the mistakes in one's own denominational history. In short, there is much that cannot and should not be received. However, through listening carefully to what we say to one another in dialogue, we hope that the Holy Spirit will enable us to discern what needs to be received for the future life of a united church.

Reconciliation — The Beginning Step

The Roman Catholic/Lutheran Joint Commission in its publication *Facing Unity* carefully noted the relationship between "reconciliation" and "reception." Reconciliation frees us "from our instinctive fear of the other as stranger and our

4. See *Facing Unity,* pp. 16–17.

anxious concern for our own identity."[5] Reconciliation always implies that we are ready to "rethink" our stereotypes about the history and doctrine of another church. This rethinking requires an openness to seeing another church's history and doctrine as legitimate expressions of the work of the Holy Spirit in the life of that church. This rethinking requires an openness to affirming that church as an authentic embodiment of Christ's Church.

Such a radical rethinking may even lead one church to appropriate what it has come to recognize in the life of another church as a gift of God for all churches. In publishing *Baptism, Eucharist and Ministry,* the Faith and Order Commission asked for such rethinking by requesting each church to consider what "guidance your church can take from this text for its worship, educational, ethical, and spiritual life and witness."[6]

Reception and Conversion

Reception requires conversion. Indeed, conversion is "as crucial to ecumenism as it is to the Christian life itself."[7] Ecumenical conversion begins with an awareness of the serious damage Christian disunity does to the proclamation of the Gospel and Christ's work in the world.

Ecumenical conversion happens because Christians talk about what unites and what divides them. A kind of conversion occurs in genuine dialogue when people really listen to one another, when their hearts become receptive to the truth that they find in each other's churches. One aspect of this conversion is a recognition that one need not defend the mistakes and errors of one's own church. Another aspect of this conversion is a freedom from the fear of being disloyal

5. *Facing Unity,* p. 22.
6. Preface, BEM.
7. Finding 2, "Ecumenical Findings: Toward a Conciliar Fellowship," *Mid-Stream* 28/1 (1989): 118.

to one's own church when one recognizes what is true and good in other churches.

Accordingly, ecumenism "does not require us . . . to betray our deepest convictions, nor to mitigate our loyalty . . . within our respective traditions"; rather, "the new insights that we receive in the graced moment of ecumenical conversion . . . enrich the truth already revealed to us and communicated through the churches of which we are members."[8]

Reception at the Local Level

Ecumenism is not meant to be only a matter of experts talking with experts. If ecumenism is really to be a vital part of the life of the church, one needs to ask what all members of the church — pastors and teachers, clergy and laity — are doing to promote ecumenism.

The basic problem in regard to ecumenical reception is that of communicating the results of ecumenical dialogue to church members at large, of helping people use ecumenical findings in their local church. In this respect, the problem of ecumenical reception is akin to communicating the decisions of the highest decision-making body of a church. All too often there is a breakdown in communication between those who teach the faith, those who preach the faith, and those who work at the ordinary business of living as committed Christians. There is a gap in the church between podium, pulpit, and pew.

Most Christians are relieved by the new climate of religious tolerance and ecumenical fellowship that has emerged during the past quarter-century. However, those who can recall a less ecumenical age when denominational loyalties loomed large and when interdenominational polemics were common may also wonder what ecumenism means in relation to their traditional belief and denominational identity. If such people are aware that agreements have been reached among

8. Finding 5, "Ecumenical Findings," p. 119.

theologians and church leaders, they do not always know how such agreements relate to their local situation nor how such agreements can help their own faith, much less lead to full, visible unity among the churches.

Reception implies a long, in-depth, and far-reaching assimilation of the ecumenical convergence developing among the churches. If the ecumenical movement is to achieve its goal of visible unity, all Christians must be involved. Accordingly, the breakdown in communication that sometimes occurs between theologians and church authorities, between pastors and parishioners, needs to be overcome.

At the local level, pastors and religious educators are sometimes unaware or uncertain of ecumenical agreements. Understandably, they may play it safe and never mention ecumenism. Ecumenism is then stifled, not through opposition but through benign neglect.[9]

However, if Christians understand that they are members not just of an institution but of a community of faith guided by the Holy Spirit who bestows gifts to different people and to different churches, then ecumenism becomes meaningful. Christians become aware that it is the will of Christ "that all may be one" (Jn. 17) and seek to make ecumenism a reality at the local level.

Christians then perceive that fidelity to Christ and the Gospel demands new attitudes, even a new direction, in the local church. Essential to the process of ecumenical reception on the local level is the involvement of pastors and lay members with their counterparts in other local churches. In other words, the study of ecumenical documents is only a background for the experience of ecumenism. Through ecumenical interaction with the clergy and laity of other churches, a genuine experience of the broader dimensions of the "whole

9. In addition to neglect, other factors that impede ecumenism are a diminished instinct for the spiritual and a lack of appreciation for the church as a pilgrim people, a community of faith, and the body of Christ.

church" can occur. Through ecumenical dialogue and activity at the local level, people soon come to a real awareness of what we share in common as Christians.

Ecumenism — A Work of the Holy Spirit

There is a saying attributed to Pierre Teilhard de Chardin: "Faith has need of the whole truth." This statement is reminiscent of the promise of Jesus: "When the Spirit of truth comes, the Spirit will guide you into all the truth" (Jn. 16:13).

This promise seems remarkably appropriate to our situation as divided Christians. The Holy Spirit enables the churches to recognize the truth of ecumenical dialogue and to discern the continuity of ecumenical statements with the teaching of the church throughout the ages, the apostolic faith. The work of bringing different denominational traditions to consensus is surely a special gift of the Holy Spirit. As the Second Vatican Council stated in its Decree on Ecumenism:

> In recent times more than ever before, He [the Lord] has been rousing divided Christians to remorse over their divisions and to a longing for unity. Everywhere large numbers have felt the impulse of this grace, and among our separated brethren also there increases from day to day the movement, fostered by the grace of the Holy Spirit, for the restoration of unity among all Christians.[10]

This and similar declarations issued by other churches are not merely instances of ecumenical rhetoric but testimonials of faith in the Spirit as the "Lord and Giver of life" who is leading the church to discover the hidden truth of its innermost unity. In other words, the Holy Spirit is given to the churches so that they will discover their unity in Christ.

10. Second Vatican Council, Decree on Ecumenism (Washington, D.C.: National Catholic Welfare Conference, 1964), pp. 1-2.

Spiritual Consequences

Granted the working of the Holy Spirit in the ecumenical movement, it is not surprising that a real desire for visible unity is gradually arising among the members of our churches. To translate this desire from idea to reality is the task and challenge of pastors and religious educators. In effect, this means that ecumenical texts such as *Baptism, Eucharist and Ministry* must be studied and taught at the local level.

Such study and teaching needs to be a kind of spiritual reading that interprets texts produced by theological dialogues in a way that is meaningful at the local level. As a practical norm for doing this, one should study such a document in the same spirit of openness in which it was written. Another practical norm is to respect the method of ecumenical dialogue in general and the purpose of this dialogue in particular.

To read a document with ecumenical openness is difficult. First of all there is the temptation to judge its statements not from the ecumenical perspective in which it was written but by comparing it with the doctrines of one's own denomination. Such a comparison is inevitably a distortion insofar as it attempts to measure an ecumenical statement by a denominational yardstick.

An ecumenical reception of an agreement such as BEM presupposes both an openness to the Holy Spirit and a willingness to allow the text to speak to us in new ways — in short, a conversion.[11] John Long has made this point well in defining

---

11. While BEM was issued to evoke some *response* from the churches and did not specifically ask for *reception* as such, it did assume an ecumenical reading of the text. Moreover, the responses given to BEM seem to be an early stage of the reception process, as is evident from the questions posed by the Faith and Order Commission about (1) "the extent to which your church can recognize in this text the faith of the Church through the ages," (2) "the consequences your church can draw from this text," and (3) "the guidance your church can take from this text" (Preface, BEM).

reception as "an understanding of what the ecumenical dialogue has accomplished and the psychological conversion which permits individuals and groups to discern what the Spirit is telling them through these accomplishments."[12]

Reception of Principles

While conversion is essential to receiving the findings of the ecumenical movement, reception is not only an affair of the heart but also a matter for the head. In other words, there are a number of key principles that churches committed to the quest for Christian unity should use in order to evaluate ecumenical proposals:

1. *Unity with Legitimate Diversity:* Reception does not mean the imposition of uniformity but the acceptance of diversity. For, as John Long has observed, diversity is not "a secondary reality merely to be tolerated but rather . . . an integral part of the inexhaustible mystery of Jesus Christ."[13] Accordingly, reception can be a reality in the life of the church only if members of one church are willing to receive the special gifts granted to other churches as gifts to be shared by the whole church.

2. *Commitment to Cooperation:* For much of their history, churches in the United States have been in competition for members and funds. Such rivalry has often given churches more the appearance of rival businesses than of witnesses of the Gospel. Churches must ask themselves "whether they are doing all they ought to do to manifest the oneness of the People of God" and "whether they should not act together in all matters except those in

12. John Long, "Reception: Ecumenical Dialogue at a Turning Point," *Ecumenical Trends* 12/2 (1983): 20.
13. Ibid.; see also Yves Congar, *Diversity and Communion* (Mystic, Conn.: Twenty-Third Publications, 1984), especially chapters 3 and 18.

which deep differences of conviction compel them to act separately."[14]

3. *Semper Reformanda* (Always to be Reforming): Like its members, the church as an institution is perennially subject to sin and thus always in need of repentance and reform. In every age, the church must be willing to repent of its unfaithfulness to the Gospel and to be open to receiving the gifts bestowed for its life and mission by the Holy Spirit.

4. *Development of Doctrine:* In preaching the Gospel to all people in every age, the church grows in its understanding of the richness of God's revelation in Christ. Thus, the church unfolds the Gospel in new and different ways under the guidance of the Holy Spirit.

5. *Hierarchy of Truths:* In proclaiming the Gospel, Christians have long recognized that some matters of revelation are more central to the Christian faith than others. In ecumenism, as in evangelism, it is vital that the fundamentals of the Gospel occupy center stage. However, as churches have explored the central mysteries of the Trinity and Incarnation, some churches have developed doctrines that have not been received by other churches.[15]

These five principles are basic to the ecumenical movement insofar as they respect the work of the Holy Spirit in the whole church throughout the ages and insofar as they enable Christians to seek the truth in charity.

---

14. "Final Report," Third World Conference on Faith and Order, Lund (Sweden), August 15–28, 1952, in *A Documentary History of the Faith and Order Movement, 1927–1963,* ed. Lukas Vischer (St. Louis, Mo.: Bethany Press, 1963), p. 86.

15. See Heinrich Fries and Karl Rahner, *Unity of the Churches: An Actual Possibility,* trans. Ruth C. L. Gritsch and Eric W. Gritsch (Philadelphia: Fortress Press; New York: Paulist Press, 1985).

The Authority of Ecumenical Texts

What is the value of bilateral statements such as the various agreements between Anglicans and Lutherans, between Reformed and Roman Catholics, etc.? What is the authority of multilateral consensus such as that expressed in BEM? Are such agreements simply an expression of a lowest common denominator of Christianity? Or the products of pragmatic bargaining? Or only the result of clever ecclesiastical diplomacy?

Or are such agreements the work of the Holy Spirit building up the church as one visible community of faith? An affirmative answer to this question does not mean that such statements are infallible or beyond critique. Such statements are necessarily provisional in character. Yet they do serve to place in perspective both the truths that Christians hold in common and the issues that still separate the churches.

In one sense, such statements have no greater authority than the people who composed them. (Such people are usually representatives of their respective churches, not official negotiators for their churches.) In another sense, such agreements are authoritative insofar as they are received by the churches. In other words, the authority of ecumenical agreements comes from their reception.

Do such statements have an "intrinsic" authority? Michael Kinnamon has spoken of moving beyond the "negotiating paradigm" to a "creative envisioning together of what we are called to be as followers of Christ." Accordingly, the intrinsic character of these statements is not formed by questions about church structures, nor by doctrinal differences, nor even by inter-church cooperation for such social concerns as justice and peace. In Kinnamon's opinion, these statements are basically intended to answer the question, "What does it mean to be the Church, living in obedience to the will of God?"[16]

16. Michael Kinnamon, "Bilaterals and the Uniting and United

In moving toward a more integrated vision of church unity, we need to remember that these ecumenical agreements take their intrinsic value from their *context* — which is the growing convergence of life and apostolic faith among the churches. This context, under the movement of the Holy Spirit, provides the texts with a kind of inspiration. As Jean-Marie Tillard has pointed out, the crucial relationship between the bilateral dialogues and the church's tradition is "the concrete and specific situation of human history."[17]

The bilateral dialogues usually begin with areas of doctrine that their participants hold in common. Yet, as John Ford has observed, each bilateral has its own integrity, "a type of authenticity that must be respected not only as integral to the bilateral process, but also as integral to eventual union." As a bilateral dialogue makes progress, the participants find divergences as well as convergences; dialogues also find areas where the doctrine or practice of one church has no obvious equivalent in another. Nonetheless, consensus is possible. In bilateral agreements, convergence obviously provides an incentive for visible unity. But even instances of divergence can have an important function as an occasion of grace that invites churches to take a leap of faith in which "the familiar and comfortable boundaries of one's present denominational horizon will need to be expanded into a more universal, and thus truly ecumenical, horizon."[18]

Another factor that gives authority to ecumenical statements such as BEM lies in the way that these statements are produced. Presently, churches have great difficulty in acting together. It is then noteworthy when churches are able to

---

Churches," *Journal of Ecumenical Studies* 23/3 (1986): 377–385, especially 380–382.

17. Jean-Marie Tillard, "The Ecclesiological Implications of Bilateral Dialogue," *Journal of Ecumenical Studies* 23/3 (1986): 412–423; see also Kortright Davis, "Bilateral Dialogue and Contextualization," in same issue, pp. 386–399.

18. John T. Ford, "Bilateral Conversations and Denominational Horizons," *Journal of Ecumenical Studies* 23/3 (1986): 518–528.

speak together with a kind of collective conscience. Consequently, BEM is not merely a joint statement; it manifests a sense of solidarity as a collegial body and growing communion between the churches.

Admittedly, there is still tension between what the churches can presently do and what still divides them. Yet a text such as BEM represents more than the spectrum of theological expertise that produced it. BEM is a testimony of churches committed to finding full, visible communion. Thus, BEM can be seen as a real, though imperfect, exercise of the future fellowship that the churches are seeking.

Such an effort to speak and act together is then an important step toward realizing the unity to which God is calling the churches. Consensus statements like BEM are the first phase of a reception process. Such statements signal the beginning of a new vision of Christian unity for members of all churches. Such statements are a promise of the time when Christians will live together in this unity and express this unity in worship and witness.[19]

Local Ecumenism

To be real, ecumenism has to be local. Reception means taking ecumenism into the blood stream of the church's life. Thus, any rationale for reception has to affirm the reality of what is happening in the local parish or congregation. Here in the life of the local church is where the *lived* experience of ecumenism must happen.[20]

Ecumenical growth does not come from the publication of ecumenical documents. Ecumenism is not only a matter of theologians sorting out doctrinal difficulties or offering theo-

---

19. It is no accident that the "Lima Liturgy" grew out of BEM, since a number of churches wanted to express the shared faith expressed in BEM through a liturgy, a formal act of worship.

20. In this respect, ecumenism resembles other spiritual movements, such as charismatic renewal, which attempt to bring new forms of life out of older ones.

logical explanations to help church authorities reach decisions about the degree of unity that is possible. Ecumenism is also the lived experience of Christians radically open to the Holy Spirit. Indeed, such experience may resolve difficulties that seem insurmountable to theologians and church leaders.

This does not mean that local ecumenism should pay scant attention to the agreements achieved by theologians and approved by church leaders. But it does mean that one cannot realistically talk about the reception of ecumenism apart from the activity of the Holy Spirit in every part of the church — in local congregations and councils of churches and in the dynamic spiritual movements of our time at the grassroots level.

It is in local ecumenism that the *sensus fidei,* the instinct for the true faith, is most active. At the local level, there is a momentum toward the unity that is communicated through the Holy Spirit. In the ecumenical interaction that takes place at the local level, the reception of ecumenical agreements take on a vitality of its own.

It is, of course, necessary for information about ecumenical progress to be communicated *to* this level. But it is even more important for theologians and church leaders to perceive the urgency for Christian unity experienced *at* this level. Theologians and church leaders need then to "receive" what the Holy Spirit is communicating through the daily experience of faithful Christians in local congregations and grassroots movements in the church.

Thus, ecumenical reception needs to take place not only from the top down — from theologians and church leaders to the main body of church members — but also from the bottom up, from the people in the pews to those in the podium and the pulpit. In other words, reception should not be *active* on the part of theologians and church leaders and *passive* on the part of the laity, but two-directional, each person giving, each person receiving.

Listening to what is going on in the life of local churches is a necessary source of inspiration for both theologians and church authorities. The whole church needs to be both a listening church and a teaching church. As Joseph Ratzinger has emphasized, local ecumenism "is not just an executive organ of centralized top level ecumenism, but rather an original form of ecumenism and an independent starting point for theological insights."[21]

Reception then is a shared experience of the unity of the whole people of God. The theological rationale for this understanding of reception is rooted in our perception of the church as a communion, as *koinonia*.[22] Reception is also rooted in *diakonia* — the "service" that the church performs in imitation of Jesus, who came not to be served but to serve (Mt. 20:26; Jn. 13:12–15; 1 Pt. 4:10). Through *koinonia* and *diakonia,* Christians are able to understand their interrelationship as a community of faith bound together by Christ.

As José Míguez Bonino has observed, theology is an imperfect yet real attempt to mediate and manifest the mystery of God in Christ. Theology therefore is both *gift* and *task*. While acknowledging that theology is a human production, Míguez Bonino also sees it as a *gift of grace* and is prompted to ask, "Are we aware, as we work theologically, of moving on ground where we have to remove our shoes?" He continues, "Have we let ourselves be so undimensionalized by modern functional . . . rationality that we are unable to give signs of our awareness of living and working 'in Christ', in the space created by the Holy Spirit?"[23]

In a comparable way, Choan-Seng Song, who considers BEM a unique, remarkable, and historic document, is quick

21. Joseph Ratzinger, "Ecumenism at the Local Level," *Information Service of the Secretariat for Promoting Christian Unity* 20 (April, 1973) II. The Secretariat is presently known as the Pontifical Council for Promoting Christian Unity.

22. The Greek term *koinonia* characterizes the intimate unity that Christ wills for his disciples; see also *Ecumenical Trends* 18/1 (1989): 1–10 and *The Ecumenical Review* 41/2 (1989): 177–183.

23. José Míguez Bonino, "The Concern for a Vital and Coherent Theology," *The Ecumenical Review* 41/2 (1989): 170.

to question whether it has "the magic power to break the 'autocephalous' nature of churches and confessions."[24] Acknowledging that the Holy Spirit is the architect of church unity, he asserts that the real test of BEM is "not in the degrees of convergence of theological and doctrinal positions . . . not even in the reception of them, but in the readiness and willingness of churches and confessions for fundamental *organic* metamorphosis, in order for these three [BEM] statements to have real *practical* impact, and in order for an *organically* united church not to remain a utopian dream."[25]

A crucial stage has been reached in the reception process. It is time for local churches to share their experience of oneness in Christ with theologians and church officials, with clergy and laity of other churches, in order to encourage the development of a *sensus fidei oecumenicae* — an instinct for an ecumenical faith. In order to become ecumenically sensitive and instinctive communities of service, local churches might consider the following suggestions:

1. A local church should be built up as a Christian community — not exclusively as a denominational institution.
2. A local church needs to keep in touch with the whole ecumenical movement so that it will continue its growth toward unity.
3. The leadership of a local church ought to create task forces in cooperation with other churches for jointly developing spiritual, ethical, and social activities in the local community.
4. Christians should honestly face doctrinal differences, while helping each other in working for a future in which all will be one.
5. Christians need to encourage a tolerance for diversity in each other's churches as they seek unity in Christ.

24. Choan-Seng Song, "The Ecumenical Calling of the Christian Church Today," *The Ecumenical Review* 41/2 (1989): 249.
25. Ibid., 249–250.

6. Local churches should seek to enter into covenants with each other by a solemn pledge to God to pursue those lines of action that enable their members to realize the ecumenical vision of one visibly united church so that "the world may believe" (Jn. 17).

14

Reception in American Culture: Tendencies and Temptations

JEFFREY GROS

The Christian community in the United States finds itself subject to several temptations relative to the Christian church. The gift of religious liberty, an experience of cultural, racial, and ethnic diversity, and a fairly young history compared with Christians of Europe all converge to make us open to a Christian identity formed by our own American principles. In brief, the identity of American Christians is different in some aspects from that of Christians of the same communion in other parts of the world.

Some Christians focus on minimal essentials, accept Americans and Christians as they are, and are reduced either to tolerance or indifference, or even the lowest common denominator in things Christian. Thus, such Christians affirm that denominational diversity is God's will and therefore not subject to reform under the Holy Spirit for the sake of the unity of the church. They may feel that the doctrine of the church is less important than faith in Christ, and therefore doctrine should not be taken so seriously as to challenge the present situations. Statistics show that many Christians apparently move from one denomination to another without any experience of religious conversion, or even without great grief about leaving behind their previous community of faith. In the past, changing churches was a traumatic experience. Some still change churches for deep reasons of conscience, but others seem to change for mere convenience. Such ecclesiological indifference is one of the great burdens on the ecumenical movement and a sign of the need for a strong religious education program in all of our churches. The churches need to communicate the biblical doctrine of church and the history of the ecumenical movement.

A second tendency among U.S. Christians is a sectarian and triumphalist one. This tendency is not indifferent to one's church but also is not open to its reform or its possibility of learning from other Christians. While affirming that Christ wills unity for the church and that there is a core of truth about the church that is central to belief in Christ, the tendency is not open to receiving truth from other Christians and does not see the urgency of Christ's call that all Christians should be one — in full communion with one another. While there is a tendency to identify this sectarian position with others, particularly those who are openly hostile to the institutions of the ecumenical movement and to some of the churches who relate to it, this type of triumphalism is possible among Orthodox, Roman Catholic, and Protestant Christians whose churches participate fully in the ecumenical movement. They see others, especially those most different from themselves, as possibly Christian, but so far from the authentic doctrine of the church that it remains impossible to imagine that anything can be learned from Christians of other traditions.

Neither of these positions — an indifference to the unity of the church or a sectarian affirmation of unity only in terms of one's own experience — is adequate to the Gospel of Jesus Christ or even to the self-understanding of many of our Christian traditions. Both of these positions are products of the search for identity in the pluralistic culture of the United States. The first allows American culture to be primary and Christian identity to be secondary. The second allows the

145

particular denominational experience of one's own church to be primary and the call of the Gospel for unity among Christians to be secondary.[1]

Both of these temptations make progress in the ecumenical movement a challenge to the Christian faith. As a Christian, each individual is called to take his or her identity in Christ as prior to the culture in which she or he lives. This requires careful Christian instruction, so that the worldwide Christian community and its history become part of one's own identity in Christ. America has a relatively short history. We tend to resolve issues practically and politically. Christianity, on the other hand, affirms the revelation of God attested to in sacred Scripture and passed on to us from the time of the Apostles through two millennia of Christian fidelity in the church. Therefore, a Christian has loyalties beyond his or her experience of congregation and denomination, of country and culture, of race and language. The reception of the ecumenical movement, first of all, necessitates a conversion to the significance of the church in our faith in Christ.

Conversion

In fact, this reception of particular ecumenical statements — whether they be about baptism or about the churches' role in the world — necessitates three levels of conversion in Christ. All Christians, if they are to bear that identity, need to be nurtured in Christ or converted to a full affirmation of his role in our salvation. When we believe in Christ, and when we focus our faith in him, we recognize all others who share this identity as more closely bound to us rather than separated by whatever it is that divides us. Christ is the ground and center of our ecumenical understanding.

Secondly, when we have received Christ and recognize all

1. These temptations are coupled with a certain lack of interest in things intellectual in American culture and the priority of professional preparation in American education.

146

who are bound to him in faith as somehow part of that reality with which we have come into communion, we cannot avoid the ecumenical ideal. That is, if we share Christ, there must be more to be shared than our present divided state. In looking into the biblical witness and the faith transmitted to us, we realize that Christ revealed a community dimension to his saving work. In reading Paul's epistles, we are admonished against the divisions that we experience in the present state of Christianity: "Is Christ divided?"[2] To be faithful to Christ, we find ourselves called to be converted to the centrality of the church in Christian existence.

The reception of the church as central to our Christian faith may be difficult in a culture that so emphasizes competition, individualism, and national identity. Conversion to the church of Christ does not necessarily lead Christians to understand their common calling to a deeper unity in the ecumenical movement. However, until the doctrine of the church becomes central to one's Christian identity and spirituality, ecumenical agreements and relationships to other Christian communities will have little importance.

U.S. Culture

Indeed in the United States one of the most painful burdens of the ecumenical movement — and what makes the reception of its results difficult — is the long history of tensions among the churches. Many Protestant collaborative efforts were developed to provide a counterbalance to Catholics immigrating to this country. Catholics and Orthodox, and occasionally Lutherans and other minority churches, have long been defending themselves against a hostile Protestant majority. African-American churches exist because of exclusion from the major Protestant traditions. The peace churches hardly

2. While it is rich in cultural and theological diversity, the New Testament witnesses that the apostolic churches were truly united in faith, worship, and mission.

survived in Europe and so have approached the wider Christian community in America with understandable suspicion. The most evident and tragic tension among Protestant Christians developed in the early twentieth century between conservative evangelicals and the historic Protestant bodies in the United States. Both communities have their own set of ecumenical agencies, journals, and institutions. However, in the pews there is a graded spectrum of opinion from the fundamentalist to the liberal, with church leadership and agencies taking positions that sometimes polarize rather than reconcile these tensions. The centrality of the doctrine of the church may be weakened in all of these groups because of the tensions that exist between Christians in the United States. Finally, the effectiveness of frontier Protestantism, with its missionary, entrepreneurial, and pioneering spirit, has made the reception of the orthodox, catholic, and historical elements of the doctrine of the church more difficult.

Conversion to a doctrine of the church, as found in history and Scripture, is also made more difficult in American culture by the implicit doctrine of progress and the emphasis on voluntary association. The Christian doctrine of sin and the biblical understanding of the universality of the church, of course, make the well-formed Christian very suspicious of any belief that progress is created by human effort. Christians are especially called to test claims of progress in their culture and nation against their understanding of God's call in the Gospel and the understanding mediated by the Christian community. It is the reception of Christian values and not the pretensions of nation or culture that should determine what is important for the Christian.

Likewise, our country has been well served by the initiatives of individuals to draw together groups in voluntary service to the society as a whole or to particular groups within it. The Red Cross, the United Way, and various civic groups continue to enrich our society. There is sometimes a temptation to allow our evaluation of fellow Christians or even of churches to be done in the context of these voluntary associations. For those unconverted to the biblical doctrine of the church, the Sunday congregation may very well be a model of a voluntary association serving the spiritual needs of its members, much as a club or lodge serves the social needs of its members. Faith in the church as integral to God's will and the action of the Spirit in the world is a much deeper evangelical commitment than can be served by a voluntary association of Christian believers. There are, of course, opportunities for voluntary organizations within a church or among churches — for study, devotions, common ministry, and the like. These, however, are subject to our understanding of Christ's will for the church. Christians believe that there is something essential in the ordained ministry, the Scripture, baptism, and the Lord's Supper, though they do not yet have a common understanding of the content of these elements essential to church life.

Individualism, voluntarism, anti-intellectualism, and a naive progressivism may be temptations for Christians in American culture. These tendencies can all be gifts if interpreted in the light of Christ's will and the biblical testimony to the centrality of community in the church. The commitment of particular individuals within the Christian community has strengthened the spirituality of American Christians in a way that is unique in the history of Christianity. The many voluntary agencies generated and sponsored by Christians have given rise not only to the ecumenical movement but also to networks of worldwide compassion without parallel in history. The willingness of frontier evangelists and congregations to forgo the intellectual rigors of a European heritage to bring Christ to the American frontier and to missions worldwide has created a force for Christianity of which we can be proud. Finally, a practical and hopeful approach to the world and to the Christian community has witnessed a resurrection faith that balances the strong — and sometimes fatalistic — emphasis on Christ's cross that so dominated Catholic and Protestant piety during the Middle Ages.

The Unity of the Church

However, none of these temptations in American culture, or even the conversion of the Christian to the centrality of Christ and the church in his or her life, represents the fullness of the Christian mystery to which American Christians are called. A third stage of conversion is necessary if the ecumenical movement is to touch the spirituality, congregational life, and teaching of our churches. As Christians we are converted to Christ and recognize all who confess him as related to us in some way. We are called to conversion in Christ to the church, the community of believers in service to God's reign. However, we are also called, on the basis of these two previous dimensions of conversion, to a commitment to the full, visible unity of the church. Otherwise our faith in the church would be a tolerant denominationalism or a triumphalist sectarianism. Both of these fall short of the biblical ideal of unity.

Reception of the ecumenical movement and conversion to God's will for the unity of the church entails four elements, all of which are a challenge in American culture. While no Christian is called to give his or her full energy to each or any one of these elements, they are dimensions of the Gospel without which the Christian community is incomplete. These elements constitute the quest for the unity to which God has called us in Christ: (1) spirituality, (2) faith, (3) common life, and (4) mission.

Faith in the one Christ calls us to faith in the church and to the churches' call to full, visible unity, treasuring the diversity of gifts of traditions and cultures. Indeed, one of the motivating forces drawing us more deeply into communion is the richness of diversity that is now denied us in our sinful and divided state. At this level of conversion, the struggles of other churches become one's own. Ecumenism is not external affairs. The internal tensions within another church do not become the opportunity to take sides but rather the challenge to internalize both sides of the conflict and seek healing.

150

We receive Christ in one another not only as individuals but as churches, recognizing the genuine differences and testing the levels of agreement necessary for these differences to be comprehended within one family.

A Receptive Spirituality

1. A *spirituality* of ecumenism will help Christians to recognize that their identity is not complete until full communion is restored. They will pray for one another, for the unity of the church, and for the renewal of their own church in response to the Gospel call. One will be enlivened by the spiritual riches of other traditions, will penetrate the spiritual life of others, and share the faith and richness of one's own tradition with the other. The themes of this volume should become spiritually exciting as resources for prayer, worship, retreats, and mutual counsel. The Spirit's impulse toward unity and the thirst for deeper levels of communion should become central to one's fidelity to Christ and to the church in which one is nurtured.

2. While scholars serve us in reconciling differences over the Christian *faith,* it is the ordinary Christian who is called to welcome and receive ecumenical formulations of faith that build the bridges that will make possible full communion in Christ. The themes treated in this volume are only a few examples of the developments that make our common understanding of church, doctrine, ethics, sacraments, and church authority more possible in our lifetime. Our life in Christ is enriched by study and reflection on ecumenical documents. Reception of new formulations of the faith that once was delivered to the apostles requires study and attentiveness on the part of Christians truly loyal to Christ's call and the biblical understanding of the church.

3. Creating a *common life* among Christians who still remain divided in certain elements of faith and sacrament

is an important witness to the faith we share, the common spirituality that is emerging, and the hope we have in the Holy Spirit for full communion. The case studies in this volume lift up some examples of common life among Christian congregations. This common life represents a depth of commitment that far exceeds the voluntary associations that are formulated for practical or devotional purposes within the churches or in society at large. Certainly these voluntary collaborative efforts may serve common life, but the level of commitment in Christ implied in the reception of his ecumenical call means that common congregational projects, covenants, or sharing witness to a reality of faith that far transcends their particular purpose.

4. Finally, the unity of the church is not only a matter of biblical fidelity to the reconciling will of God in Christ. It is also a response to God's call for common *mission* in the world. A church divided at the Lord's Table or in the ordained ministry is a scandal to the world and an inhibition to the preaching of the Gospel of Jesus Christ. A Christian community charged with service to God's justice, peace, and integrity of creation is diminished in its ability to do so by its lack of visible unity and the inability of the Christian family to speak with one voice about values so central to the Gospel witness. Faith in the Gospel of Jesus Christ should stimulate all Christians to transcend their individualism and the ever present temptation to allow the mission of the Gospel to be polarized by various political priorities. Indeed, Christians are called to confer together most especially when they have different positions on their priorities in mission to the world. The bond of Christ should hold together the most diverse of ethnic, racial and cultural differences.

There are many temptations in American culture that fragment Christians. The Faith and Order movement's call to reconciliation in doctrine, sacraments, life, and mission in such a way that in Christ our differences can be seen as gifts is difficult in American culture. An intellectual approach to the tensions that alienate us, conversion beyond tolerance and voluntary affiliation, openness of all of our churches (with all of their gifts) to genuine renewal and reform under the influence of the Holy Spirit — all of these challenges can only become a reality with prayer, study, and fasting as we respond to God's grace for the church. It is hoped that this small volume will be a useful resource for the reception of ecumenical developments in the churches through the power of the Holy Spirit.

15

Reception at the Local and Regional Levels

FRANK H. DIETZ

In the early church, "reception" was the process by which decisions of local and regional councils gradually came to be accepted throughout the *oikoumene* — the known world of that day. Such a process took an immense amount of time and effort: First, the available means of communication were slow; it took a long time for a letter to travel from Jerusalem to Alexandria, or from Antioch to Rome. Secondly, people in different parts of the ancient world had different languages, different cultures, and even different theologies; thus, the meaning of a decision taken in one church might not be immediately understood, much less readily accepted, by people in a distant church. Still a third factor in reception stemmed from the fact that conciliar decisions were usually formulated by a select group of clergy and thus needed to be communicated to and received by the laity.[1]

Similar problems of reception exist today. While modern technology makes communication around the world almost

1. For a succinct overview of reception, see William G. Rusch, *Reception: An Ecumenical Opportunity* (Philadelphia: Fortress Press, 1987).

instantaneous, time is still needed for decisions taken in one part of the world to make a real impact elsewhere. In other words, reception really requires more than mere information about a decision; true reception needs a thoughtful process of education and reflection.

Secondly, while the world has become more accustomed to pluralism, there is still a tendency to judge ecumenical proposals not in virtue of their intrinsic merits but in light of one's own denominational tradition. Genuine reception, however, requires us to move beyond sectarian denominationalism to ecumenical convergence.

Thirdly, tension still remains between the thinking of theologians on the one hand and the concerns of church leaders on the other. In addition, there is sometimes tension between church leaders, theologians, and people at the local level; it is quite possible for these three groups to move in three different directions. Thus, authentic reception requires interaction between podium, pulpit, and pew.

Given such factors, can reception ever become a reality at the local level? The answer is emphatically "yes!" — at least that is the experience of the Texas Conference of Churches. By sharing some of its experience, it is hoped that other ecumenical conferences, councils, and coalitions — at last report, there were some 650 such organizations in the United States — will be encouraged to share their own experiences of reception and to undertake new ventures in the ecumenical pilgrimage.[2]

As one might anticipate, reception has taken a rich variety of forms in different places. From this wealth of experience, one can only share a few samples, arranged as follows: (1) The Texas Conference of Churches, (2) Convergence in Worship, (3) Reception of *Baptism, Eucharist and Ministry,* (4) Theological Dialogue, (5) Grassroots Ecumenism, and (6) Reception: Work of the Spirit.

---

2. This information was provided by Ecumenical Networks of the National Council of Churches.

FRANK H. DIETZ

The Texas Conference of Churches

In proverbial Texas fashion, much could and should be said about the ecumenical effort among the churches. For present purposes, two brief remarks must suffice.

First, the Texas Conference of Churches is a conciliar partnership of fifty-one judicatories or governing units representing sixteen different communions. The present structure of the conference dates from the time of the Second Vatican Council (1962–65), when all of the Roman Catholic dioceses of Texas joined with an existing statewide council of churches, consisting of Protestant and Orthodox groups, to create a new ecumenical organization. Since its founding, the Texas Conference of Churches has included a Life and Work component (known as the Commission of Church and Society of the Texas Conference of Churches) that fosters discussions about, and cooperation in, social projects, such as those concerned with justice and peace. Right from the start, the Texas Conference has also held annual faith and order meetings that have featured nationally and internationally known ecumenists. This Faith and Order Conference is in the larger context of the work of the Commission for Christian Unity and Interfaith Relations. Consequently, the discussion of doctrinal topics, such as that presented in *Baptism, Eucharist and Ministry* is not new to the conference.

Secondly, parallel and complementary to these efforts, discussions are fostered by the Consultation on Church Union (COCU), which has recently called upon its participant churches to enter into a covenant.[3]

3. COCU was established in 1962 for promoting union discussions among four major churches — the Episcopal, Methodist, and (northern) Presbyterian churches, and the United Church of Christ; subsequently other churches joined these discussions. In addition to the original churches (two of which, the United Methodist and the Presbyterian, have had further unions), current participants include the Disciples of Christ, African Methodist Episcopal Church, African Methodist Epis-

Clergy and laity from the nine churches have engaged in a variety of conversations about the proposed COCU covenanting.[4] But in addition to the discussions of the covenant proposal among members of the participating churches, Lutheran, Orthodox, and Roman Catholic leaders convened a conference to examine the consensus developing among their COCU colleagues.[5]

Convergence in Worship

Such discussions have created interest, not only about what other churches believe, but also about how they worship. In local congregations, adult education groups have studied the histories, doctrines, and traditions of other churches and then visited these churches for worship. Frequently these visitors discovered that "in the essentials we are so much alike."

In some instances, such visits have led members of local churches to rediscover forgotten aspects of their own traditions. As one pastor commented, "We came to realize that some of the services used material in our own denominational worship that we had ignored for years." In other instances, such visits persuaded members of one church to "borrow" elements from the services of other churches for use in their own worship.

Thus, through study and sharing there has been an unanticipated convergence in worship, so that it is not unusual to find churches borrowing symbols and ceremonies from each other for use both in the regular Sunday worship as well as for special services such as ordination and installations. In

---

copal Zion Church, Christian Methodist Church, and the International Council of Community Churches.

4. Among other documents, see Gerald F. Moede, ed., *The COCU Consensus: In Quest of a Church of Christ Uniting* and *Covenanting Toward Unity: From Consensus to Communion* (Princeton, N.J.: COCU, 1985).

5. Similarly, in Minnesota, Lutheran and Roman Catholic leaders came together to discuss the work of COCU.

both the rediscovery of forgotten practices and the borrowing from other traditions, there is a process of mutual liturgical enrichment, a process of reception at work.

At the local level, this process has led to many discussions about the possibility of concelebrating the eucharist. In some instances, this has been officially approved, as in the case of joint liturgies sponsored by the member churches of COCU. In other instances, where official approval has not been given for eucharistic concelebration, there have been public services of repentance for the continued existence of denominational barriers — sometimes in dramatic fashion. For example, some groups have set the eucharistic table and prayed for the time when all Christians can approach that table together but then concluded the service with a painful confession of the brokenness and disunity that still make it impossible for all Christians to share the eucharist together.

In many areas it has become customary for churches to join together in prayer. Some special occasions are Thanksgiving and the Week of Prayer for Christian Unity. In addition, some local churches have found other innovative ways to express their growing sense of unity. For example, in some places, churches of different traditions meet for weekly public worship on the town square or village green. And in one community in West Virginia, a group of churches declared themselves to be "the church" of that community.[6]

Reception of BEM

Like many other regional ecumenical groups, the Texas Conference of Churches made a commitment to study BEM. With the aid of a former staff member of the World Council of Churches, the board of directors of the Texas Conference began studying the historical development of BEM and its implications for their churches.

6. Avery Post, unpublished keynote address, National Workshop on Christian Unity, Pittsburgh, Penn., May 1990.

The Texas Conference also sponsored several special workshops that brought together the ecumenical officers of the churches and faculty members from various seminaries in the state. These discussions were particularly useful for those ecumenical officers who were involved in formulating their churches' responses to BEM. For other participants, these discussions helped sharpen the key issues emerging out of BEM. Those who attended these workshops were in turn able to encourage discussions of BEM at the local level. The result at the grassroots level was an in-depth discussion of BEM, both within and between local congregations of different denominational traditions. Thus, BEM began to be seen as the real expression of a partnership far beyond what its writers might have envisioned.

Similar discussions about BEM took place during the annual Faith and Order meetings sponsored by the Texas Conference of Churches. Many participants were soon ready to move from the consensus expressed in BEM to concrete action at the grassroots level. Some began to challenge the leadership of the Texas Conference to move beyond its accustomed agenda into new initiatives. Others found in BEM a theological consensus for concelebration of the eucharist and mutual recognition of ministries.

For example, at one meeting the suggestion was made that the "Lima Liturgy," which grew out of BEM, should be used at the annual statewide assembly and that following pre-communion the delegates be divided into three groups, separated from one another by the dividers in the meeting room. After prayers expressing a new sense of community and a willingness to move beyond the traditional, the dividers would be used so that all would celebrate the eucharist at the same time, though separately as still required by their traditions. This suggestion was never implemented. The Texas Conference considers its "official functions" inappropriate to force "breakthroughs" — however ecumenically popular — until these are authorized by the member churches. Such suggestions serve to illustrate the growing desire for removing all barriers to eucharistic sharing.

Likewise, the study of BEM has produced a strong affirmation of one another's ministries, thereby suggesting that people are ready for an "official reconciliation of ministries." Even before this is given, there are signs of a kind of "unofficial" recognition manifested by the greater willingness of people from one church to attend the ordinations and installations of clergy and officials in other churches. One ordained pastor serves Episcopal and Lutheran parishes according to a covenant between the Episcopal and Lutheran bishops.

In effect, there is a growing desire to see the consensus on the eucharist and ministry that is voiced in BEM put into practice at the local level. For some people, the reception of BEM has already gone much beyond the text itself.

Theological Dialogue

Some have claimed that theological discussions, such as those that produced BEM, are the preserve of academics and thus far removed from the grassroots level. There is truth to this claim insofar as there is still a need for the theological efforts of the bilateral and multilateral dialogues to be shared at the local level. Nonetheless, ecumenical agreements — if appropriately written and effectively communicated — do receive a widespread and enthusiastic reception on the local level. For example, a half-dozen years after the publication of BEM, "about 350,000 copies have been circulated all over the world in 35 languages — and more translations are still in the making."[7]

This experience shows that ecumenical agreements such as BEM have the potential to enhance, empower, and even change the way that churches express themselves, both intramurally and ecumenically. From a psychological viewpoint, frequently it is only in dialogue with others that a

---

7. Max Thurian, ed., *Churches Respond to BEM: Official Response to the "Baptism, Eucharist and Ministry" Text,* Volume VI, Faith and Order Paper 144 (Geneva: World Council of Churches, 1988), p. ix.

person achieves a better self-understanding. Correspondingly, ecumenical dialogue can help churches broaden their self-understanding and so foster better relationships with other local churches. In other words, the better understanding members of a church have of their own denominational heritage, the better prepared they are to engage in dialogue with others.

Just as individuals may need professional assistance in order to achieve greater self-understanding and to improve their relationships with others, so, too, churches may be helped by theological professionals. In Texas, for example, a number of theological seminaries provided resource persons for the interpretation of the history of the Faith and Order movement of the World Council of Churches.

Thus, the reception of BEM was aided by scholars who were available both to interpret BEM and to relate it to the denominational backgrounds of different churches. In addition, many of these faculty members already had some experience in ecumenical dialogue. This combination of experience and expertise was a valuable asset in providing both clergy and laity with an understanding of the implications of BEM for their local congregations.[8]

In other words, theological dialogue has an important role to play on the local level.

Grassroots Ecumenism

In addition to statewide events, there has been a rich variety of endeavors on the local level, as rich and varied as the landscape of Texas itself, which ranges from wide rural expanses to ultra-modern metropolitan areas. Two examples, one metropolitan, the other rural, may help to indicate what has happened and to suggest possibilities for the future.

---

8. These seminaries, and other institutions such as the Institute for Religion at the Houston Medical Center, provided educational opportunities for clergy who wished to study the implications of BEM.

Reception of BEM received a major impetus when the then director of the Greater Dallas Community of Churches challenged its board — which represented an impressively diverse group of local churches — to find ways to allow BEM to inform their local relationships. The board accepted the challenge by (1) holding an ecumenical retreat for key local leaders, (2) developing strategies to involve congregations throughout the Dallas area in the study of BEM, (3) sponsoring lectures by visiting ecumenists and faculty members from local seminaries, and (4) arranging a metropolitan celebration of the Lima Liturgy — which was attended by high-ranking church leaders.

As an integral part of this multifaceted endeavor, strong efforts were made to ensure racial and ethnic inclusiveness and the participation of the leaders of as many different denominations as possible. Similarly, the discussion of BEM brought together an unusual blend of people at the grassroots level. On the one hand, a series of seminars was held in conjunction with an already existing volunteer ministry program at community colleges. On the other hand, people from a surprising number of congregations participated in discussions at cluster-sites.

In evaluating this process, what looms largest in importance is the preparation of the leaders. In those instances where the local resource people were not well prepared, participants in the seminars expressed dissatisfaction. Unfortunately, the same proved true with the homilist at the Lima Liturgy, who made a number of unhelpful and seemingly uninformed remarks about the "real presence" in the elements of the eucharist. In effect, the homily provided more confusion than inspiration, but, as some commented, it did inspire people to reread BEM to see what it really says about the eucharist.

In a metropolitan area, there are many resources available. However, to utilize these resources well, considerable attention must be given to excellent communication and good education; otherwise, the best designed plans can only suffer and the desired level of reception will not be reached.

Rural areas, in contrast, offer a different set of challenges. For example, a study group of about a dozen ministers in a rural area used BEM as the basis for nearly two years of biweekly study sessions. Participants prepared papers on baptism, eucharist, and ministry that compared the viewpoint of their own denominational traditions and that of BEM. Even though participants were not equally qualified academically to deal with some of the issues, the conversations were fascinating and characterized by patience and openness.

Periodically, someone would demand, "Why not get on with common ministries?" or "Why not celebrate the eucharist together?" While this did not happen, other results gradually became evident: the participants began to prepare their sermons and liturgies in light of the discussions that had taken place in their study group. A sense of partnership developed across denominational lines; some participants commented that their occasional meals together took on a eucharistic flavor.

Such experiences seem likely to occur in rural areas. For example, in another local discussion group among clergy in a small community, one pastor observed, "After spending time together on the ministry section, we determined there were some key outreach ministries to do together. Putting them together has multiplied rather than dissipated energies. The children of our community are better for it."

From the viewpoint of reception, it is important to note that many of the issues that emerged in these rural discussion groups are reflected in the official responses that the churches made to BEM.[9] Moreover, the pastors and priests who participated in these groups seem to have recognized a new and deeper unity that surpassed what was articulated in the official responses to BEM. Indeed, ecumenical groups of rural clergy seem to sense a partnership in their local setting greater than that authorized or acknowledged by officials of their different churches.[10]

---

9. See the six volumes of *Churches Respond to BEM*.
10. The information provided here is derived from personal contact.

FRANK H. DIETZ

Reception: Work of the Spirit

From a variety of personal ecumenical experiences, two important impressions about reception emerge.

First, it is evident that local clergy and laity are often energized by their ecumenical contacts and want to share such experiences by initiating ecumenical programs and projects in their parishes. Such local leaders sense that the churches are truly one and so are called to a common table and a shared ministry; these leaders generally want to remove the historical and doctrinal barriers to unity as quickly as possible. These leaders want to build bridges across the chasms of separation without further delay. On the one hand is a sense of enthusiasm in discovering the underlying closeness between Christians. On the other hand is a feeling of frustration that union among Christians is moving so slowly.

Secondly, it is evident that local clergy and laity are already being mutually enriched by a "sharing of gifts" — a phrase that has become common in local ecumenical circles. In ecumenical groups there is the deep conviction — a *sensus fidelium* — that we are not only the heirs of the treasures of our own traditions, but we are called to be sharers of our spiritual gifts with one another. Thus, reception is a reciprocal process of enriching and being enriched.

If the Spirit is at work in creating such gifts, is not the Spirit also at work in the creative sharing of such gifts? How else can we account for the energy and enthusiasm that churches experience in sharing with each other the charisms that they have received?

A Selected Bibliography

JEFFREY GROS AND JOHN T. FORD

DOCUMENTS

Baptism, Eucharist and Ministry. Faith and Order Paper 111. Geneva: World Council of Churches, 1982. This document, approved by the Faith and Order Commission at Lima, Peru, in 1982, is the most far-reaching consensus achieved to date by theologians from a broad spectrum of churches. This document has been translated into dozens of languages and reprinted in many places.

Kinnamon, Michael, ed. *Towards Visible Unity: Commission on Faith and Order, Lima, 1982.* Volume I, Faith and Order Paper 112, Minutes and Addresses. Volume II, Faith and Order Paper 113, Study Papers and Reports. Geneva: World Council of Churches, 1982, 1983. These two volumes, which include the proceedings and papers from the meeting of the Faith and Order Commission at Lima in 1982, are primarily of interest to people doing theological research.

Thurian, Max and Geoffrey Wainwright, eds. *Baptism and Eucharist: Ecumenical Convergence in Celebration,* Faith and Order Paper 117. Geneva: World Council of

165

Churches; Grand Rapids: Eerdmans, 1983. This is a very useful volume for theologians and liturgists who wish to compare recent baptismal and eucharist texts from a spectrum of different churches.

Thurian, Max, ed. *Churches Respond to BEM*. 6 vols. Geneva: World Council of Churches, 1986–1988. These volumes contain the official responses from dozens of churches to the questions posed by the Lima document.

COMMENTARIES

Fahey, Michael A., ed., *Catholic Perspectives on Baptism, Eucharist and Ministry: A Study Commissioned by the Catholic Theological Society of America*. Lanham, Md.: University Press of America, 1986. This volume, prepared as a team project by five Roman Catholic theologians, indicates a basically favorable reception along with some proposals for future consideration.

Lazareth, William H. *Growing Together in Baptism, Eucharist and Ministry: A Study Guide*. Faith and Order Paper 114. Geneva: World Council of Churches, 1982. This booklet, which contains outlines of each of the topics along with discussion questions, is useful for study groups.

Limouris, Gennadios and Nomikos Michael Vaporis, eds. *Orthodox Perspectives on Baptism, Eucharist and Ministry,* Faith and Order Paper 128. Brookline, Mass.: Holy Cross Orthodox Press, 1985. This volume of papers from the Inter-Orthodox Symposium is valuable for showing that Orthodox theologians viewed BEM with considerable acceptance yet with some important reservations.

Seils, Michael, ed. *Lutheran Convergence? An Analysis of the Lutheran Responses to the "Baptism, Eucharist and Ministry" Text*. Geneva: Lutheran World Federation, 1988.

Thurian, Max, ed. *Ecumenical Perspectives on Baptism, Eucharist and Ministry,* Faith and Order Paper 116. Geneva: World Council of Churches, 1983. This book of fifteen essays related to the Lima document is primarily of interest to people with some theological training.

STUDIES ON RECEPTION

Alberigio, G., J. P. Jossua, and J. Komonchak, *The Reception of Vatican II*. Washington: The Catholic University of America Press, 1987.

Congar, Yves. "Reception as an Ecclesiological Reality," *Election and Consensus in the Church,* ed. Giuseppe Alberigio and Anton Weiler, *Concilium* 77. New York: Herder and Herder, 1972, pp. 43–68.

Gros, Jeffrey. "Reception and Beyond." *Ecumenical Trends* 14/1 (1985): 6–8.

————. "Reception of the Ecumenical Movement in the Roman Catholic Church with Special Reference to *Baptism, Eucharist and Ministry,*" *American Baptist Quarterly* 7/1 (1988): 38–49.

Lossky, Nicholas, et al., eds. *Dictionary of the Ecumenical Movement*. Geneva: WCC Publications, 1991. S.V. "Reception," by Anton Houtepen. See also other entries relevant to the topic.

Marthaler, Berard L., ed. *New Catholic Encyclopedia*. Vol. 18. Washington, D.C.: The Catholic University of America Press, 1989. See especially Jeffrey Gros, "Faith and Order Commission"; John F. Hotchkin, "Ecumenical Dialogues"; John Reumann, "Lutherans in Dialogue"; Darlis J. Swan, "Evangelical Lutheran Church in America"; as well as other related articles.

Rausch, Thomas P. "Reception Past and Present." *Theological Studies* 47/3 (1986): 497–508.

Rusch, William G. *Reception: An Ecumenical Opportunity*. Philadelphia: Fortress Press, 1987. This short book provides a useful overview of the current discussion on the theological implications of "reception."

Sullivan, Emmanuel. "Reception: Factor and Moment in Ecumenism." *Ecumenical Trends* 15/7 (1986): 105–110; responses by Protestant, Evangelical, and Roman Catholic ecumenists in the same issue, pp. 111–118.

Tillard, J. M. R. "Reception: A Time to Beware of False Steps." *Ecumenical Trends* 14/11 (1985): 145–148.

———. "Did we 'receive' Vatican II?" *One in Christ* 21/4 (1985): 276–283.

AMERICAN CHURCHES

Current information about American Christianity and American churches is available in the following publications:

Dictionary of Christianity in America. Downers Grove, Ill.: Intervarsity Press, 1990.

The Encyclopedia of American Religion. Detroit: Gale Research, 1989.

Shriver, Peggy L. *Having Gifts That Differ: Profiles of Ecumenical Churches.* New York: Friendship Press, 1989.

Yearbook of American and Canadian Churches. Prepared annually by the National Council of the Churches of Christ in the United States of America. Nashville: Abingdon Press.

THE CONSULTATION ON CHURCH UNION

Covenanting Toward Unity: From Consensus to Communion, A Proposal to the Churches from the Consultation on Church Union. Princeton, N.J.: Consultation on Church Union, 1985.

Crow, Paul A., Jr., and William Jerry Boney, eds. *Church Union at Midpoint.* New York: Association Press, 1972.

Crow, Paul A., Jr. *Christian Unity: Matrix for Mission.* New York: Friendship Press, 1982.

Ford, John T. "A Plan and a Process: the Pilgrimage of the

Consultation on Church Union." *The Jurist* 44 (1984): 247–275.

Moede, Gerald F. *The COCU Consensus: In Quest of a Church of Christ Uniting.* Princeton, N.J.: Consultation on Church Union, 1985.

———. *Oneness in Christ: The Quest and the Questions.* Princeton, N.J.: Consultation on Church Union, 1981.

A Roster of Churches and Ecumenical Organizations

PAUL WALSH

The following roster is provided for convenience in identifying the churches and ecclesiastical organizations mentioned in the text; further information about these and other
American churches may be found in the books listed in the
bibliography under the heading "American Churches."

African Methodist Episcopal Church (AME) was established
as a distinct African-American denomination in 1816
under the leadership of Bishop George Allen in protest
against the racial discrimination of the Methodist Episcopal Church in Philadelphia.

African Methodist Episcopal Zion Church (AMEZ) traces its
origin to 1796, when Philip Embury led in the formation
of a separate African American congregation in protest
against the racial discrimination of the Methodist Episcopal Church in New York.

American Baptist Churches in the U.S.A., whose present name
dates from 1972, was previously known as the American
Baptist Convention (1950) but traces its history back
through the Northern Baptist Convention to colonial

times in America and to the Separatist movement in England at the end of the sixteenth century.

American Lutheran Church (ALC) was established as the result of several mergers, first of Lutheran synods of predominantly German background in 1930 and later of churches of Norwegian and Danish origin in the 1960s; the ALC united with the Lutheran Church in America (LCA) and the Association of Evangelical Lutheran Churches (AELC) to form the Evangelical Lutheran Church in America (ELCA) in 1987.

Anglican Communion is a worldwide association of autonomous regional churches that share historical links and traditions of worship and governance with the Church of England and are presently in communion with the Archbishop of Canterbury; the Episcopal Church in the United States is a member of the Anglican Communion.

Anglican-Roman Catholic International Commission (ARCIC) is a bilateral theological dialogue officially sponsored by the Anglican Communion and the Roman Catholic Church.

Association of Evangelical Lutheran Churches (AELC) was formed as an "interim denomination" in 1969 as the result of dissatisfaction with the conservative orientation of the Lutheran Church–Missouri Synod; in 1987, the AELC joined with the American Lutheran Church (ALC) and the Lutheran Church in America (LCA) to form the Evangelical Lutheran Church in America (ELCA).

Baptist World Alliance is a voluntary association of various Baptist unions and conventions that was established in 1905 as a forum for education, evangelization, and world aid.

Christian Church (Disciples of Christ) began on the American Frontier as an ecumenical movement that held that the unity of the church is essential for mission and evangelism; loosely organized in 1832, the Church adopted its present organizational structure in 1968.

Christian Methodist Episcopal Church (CME) was formed in 1870 as an African-American Church distinct from, yet with the support of, the Methodist Episcopal Church South.

Church of God in Christ, a church in the Pentecostal tradition, was first established in 1894 in Jackson, Mississippi, by Charles H. Mason; there are also churches with similar names that have split from the main body.

Consultation on Church Union (COCU) was established in 1962 for promoting union discussions among four major churches (Episcopal, Methodist, Presbyterian, and the United Church of Christ); other churches subsequently joined this quest for unity so that, in addition to the original four, current members include the Disciples of Christ, three African-American Churches (AME, AMEZ, CME) and the International Council of Community Churches (ICCC).

Disciples Ecumenical Consultative Council is an international body established in 1975 as a means of promoting deeper fellowship between the Disciples of Christ and other Christians through encouraging participation in the ecumenical movement.

Episcopal Church (EC) was organized as a separate church after the American Revolution by members of the Church of England; like other members of the Anglican Communion, the EC uses the *Book of Common Prayer* in its liturgy.

Evangelical Lutheran Church in America (ELCA) was formed in 1987 through a merger of three Lutheran Churches (AELC, ALC, LCA) and now includes 5.3 million Lutherans in the United States.

Evangelical United Brethren (EUB) was formed in 1946 through the union of the Evangelical Church and the United Brethren in Christ; in 1968, the EUB united with the Methodist Church to form the United Methodist Church.

Faith and Order Commission of the World Council of

Churches (F&O) traces its origin to an ecumenical meeting at Lausanne, Switzerland, in 1927; in 1948, it joined with the Life and Work movement to form the World Council of Churches (WCC). F&O continues as a distinct commission within the WCC and is responsible for producing statements of theological convergence.

Working Group on Faith and Order of the National Council of Churches (WGF&O) is a body within the National Council that encourages ecumenical dialogue between the churches (both members and non-members) and prepares theological statements for consideration by the ecumenical community.

The Greek Orthodox Archdiocese of North and South America was established in 1922 under the jurisdiction of the Patriarch of Constantinople.

International Council of Community Churches was organized in 1950 as a fellowship of community churches committed to Christian unity; these congregationally governed churches arose in the nineteenth century particularly in communities too small to support more than one church.

Lutheran Church in America (LCA) was established in 1962 and brought together synods of German, Swedish, Finnish, and Danish background; in 1987, the LCA united with the American Lutheran Church (ALC) and the Association of Evangelical Lutheran Churches (AELC) to form the Evangelical Lutheran Church in America (ELCA).

Lutheran World Federation (LWF) is a communion of Lutheran churches in all parts of the world. Founded in Lund, Sweden, in 1947, the LWF now has 106 member churches representing some 55 million of the world's 59 million Lutherans.

National Baptist Convention of the United States of America, Incorporated, is an organization of predominantly black churches that dates back to 1895, when three Baptist groups merged to form the National Baptist Convention of the U.S.A., Inc.; a major split occurred in 1915, when a group left to form the National Baptist Convention of America.

National Council of Churches of Christ in the U.S.A. (NCCC) "is a community of Christian communions which in response to the gospel as revealed in the scriptures, confess Jesus Christ, the incarnate Word of God, as Savior and Lord." Established in 1950, as the successor to the Federal Council of Churches, the NCCC currently numbers thirty-two churches among its members.

Orthodox Church in America (OCA) traces its origin to 1794, when the Russian Orthodox Church established a mission in Alaska; the OCA achieved its present canonical structure in 1970, with the union of Orthodox jurisdictions, not only of Russian but also of Albanian, Bulgarian, and Romanian background.

Presbyterian Church (U.S.A.) (PC) was established in 1983 with the union of two previously independent northern (United Presbyterian Church in the United States of America) and southern (Presbyterian Church in the United States) churches, which had separated before the Civil War.

Reformed Church in America (RCA) adopted its present name in 1867, although its origins go back to 1628, when the first Reformed church was established in New Amsterdam (New York), which was then under Dutch rule.

Roman Catholic Church (RCC) was first organized in the United States with the creation of the Diocese of Baltimore in 1789; while under the authority of the Bishop of Rome, Roman Catholics in the United States are led by the National Conference of Catholic Bishops.

Southern Baptist Convention, the largest Baptist body in the United States, was founded in Augusta, Georgia, in 1845 as a result of the tensions that would later lead to war between the North and South. The Southern Baptist Convention has become the largest Protestant body in the United States.

United Church of Christ (UCC) was constituted in 1957 by the union of the Congregational Christian Church and the Evangelical and Reformed Church, both of which resulted from church mergers in the 1930s.

United Methodist Church (UMC) traces its history back to a gathering of Wesleyan preachers who formed the Methodist Episcopal Church in Baltimore in 1784; after a reunion of the major branches of Methodism in 1939, the UMC was formed in 1968, through union with the Evangelical United Brethren.

World Alliance of Reformed Churches (WARC) is a confederation of some 169 autonomous churches in the Presbyterian and Congregational tradition.

World Council of Churches (WCC) is a fellowship of over three hundred churches that confess the Lord Jesus Christ as Savior. With headquarters in Geneva, Switzerland, the WCC was formed at Amsterdam in 1948 as the result of the merger of two earlier ecumenical movements: Faith and Order and Life and Work.

World Methodist Council (WMC) is an association of some sixty-four different Methodist churches and groups; originating in 1881, the WMC endeavors to foster Methodist involvement in education, evangelism, and ecumenism.

Contributors

FRANK H. DIETZ, Th.D. (United Church of Christ) is Executive Director of the Texas Conference of Churches, Austin, Texas.

JOHN T. FORD, S.T.D. (Roman Catholic) is Professor of Theology at The Catholic University of America, Washington, D.C.

AURELIA T. FULE, Th.D. (Presbyterian Church, U.S.A.) is Associate for Faith and Order, Theology and Worship Unit, Presbyterian Church, U.S.A., Louisville, Kentucky.

JULIA GATTA, Ph.D. (Episcopal Church) is Vicar of St. Paul's Parish, Windham, Connecticut.

JEFFREY GROS, Ph.D. (Roman Catholic) is Associate Director, Secretariat for Ecumenical and Interreligious Affairs, National Conference of Catholic Bishops, Washington, D.C.

DALE JAMTGAARD, M.S.W. (Evangelical Lutheran Church in America) is pastor of the Mission of the Atonement, Beaverton, Oregon.

ROGER OLSON, Ph.D. (Baptist General Conference) is Associate Professor of Theology at Bethel College, Minnesota.

GAIL M. REYNOLDS, M.Div. (United Church of Christ) is Associate Conference Minister of the South Central Conference of the United Church of Christ.

MICHAEL ROGNESS, Th.D. (Evangelical Lutheran Church in America) is Associate Professor, Luther Northwestern Theological Seminary, St. Paul, Minnesota.

EMMANUEL SULLIVAN, Ph.D. (Roman Catholic) is ecumenical officer of the Diocese of Arundel and Brighton (United Kingdom).

DARLIS J. SWAN, Ph.D. (Evangelical Lutheran Church in America) is Associate Director, Department for Ecumenical Affairs of the Evangelical Lutheran Church in America, Chicago, Illinois.

NEHEMIAH THOMPSON, Ph.D. (United Methodist Church) is Associate General Secretary of the General Commission on Christian Unity and Interreligious Concerns.

PATRICK VISCUSO, Ph.D. (Greek Orthodox) is a priest of the Greek Orthodox Church.

PAUL WALSH, M.Div. (Roman Catholic) is a doctoral student in the Department of Theology at The Catholic University of America, Washington, D.C.

RENA M. YOCOM, D.Min. (United Methodist) is Associate General Secretary of the Mission Education and Cultivation Program Department of the United Methodist Church, New York.

APPRECIATION

In addition to the contributors listed above, special appreciation goes to others who assisted in the preparation of this book: members and guests of the Faith and Order Working Group, members of local churches and councils of churches, and theological students who discussed and critiqued different parts of the book in the course of its preparation; and to Delene Costante of the Department for Ecumenical Affairs in the Evangelical Lutheran Church in America, who typed the final manuscript.